Eternal Promises, Eternal Home

A Study of Heaven:
The City That is to Come

Matthew Allen

Published by
Spiritbuilding Publishers
9700 Ferry Road
Waynesville, OH 45068

ETERNAL PROMISES, ETERNAL HOME
A Study of Heaven: The City That Is to Come
By Matthew Allen

ISBN 978–1–964–80560–3

Spiritbuilding
PUBLISHERS

spiritbuilding.com

Table of Contents

Preface

Heaven has always captivated the hearts of God's people. From the days of Abraham, who "was looking forward to the city that has foundations," to the exiled John, who saw the New Jerusalem descending from heaven, the promise of our eternal home has given strength to believers in every generation.

This study, *Eternal Promises, Eternal Home,* was written to help us focus on that hope. Life in this world is full of uncertainty, loss, and sorrow. But Scripture reminds us that the story doesn't end here. The final pages of the Bible reveal a world where every tear is wiped away, death is no more, and God Himself dwells among His people.

Each lesson in this series explores a different aspect of that eternal home: the beauty of the city, the presence of God, the joy of His people, and the life that never ends. These chapters are not meant to satisfy our curiosity about heaven's details but to renew our faith in God's promises. The goal is not just to imagine heaven but to live now as citizens of that coming world.

My prayer is that these lessons will steady your heart, strengthen your hope, and remind you that the best is yet to come. Whatever you face in this life, remember: God is not finished. He is preparing a place for His people, and one day, the voice from the throne will say, "It is done."

Until that day, let us live with faith, walk with endurance, and look forward to the home of the soul.

Matthew Allen
September 2025

Introduction

From the first pages of Scripture to the last, God shows Himself as a promise-keeping God. Every covenant, every act of deliverance, and every word of hope points to a single goal: bringing His people home. The Bible begins with creation marred by sin and ends with creation restored in glory. Between those two scenes, the story of redemption unfolds.

For Christians, heaven isn't just an abstract idea or a faraway dream. It is the fulfillment of everything God has planned and promised. Jesus described it as a real place prepared for His followers: a home where sorrow, death, and fear will never exist again. Revelation 21 and 22 reveal that home and show us what awaits: a city shining with God's glory, a river of life flowing from His throne, and the redeemed gathered in perfect joy.

This study, *Eternal Promises, Eternal Home*, follows that vision. Each lesson takes us deeper into the promises of God revealed in His word. Together, we will trace how heaven completes His work of grace, how His presence defines our eternal joy, and how His promises shape how we live right now.

These lessons are designed not just to inform, but to encourage. They remind us that heaven is not far away; it is the destination of every faithful heart. The hope of our eternal home gives meaning to the present, strength in trial, and courage to keep walking by faith.

As we study, remember: heaven is not the reward of the righteous; it is the gift of the Redeemer. And one day, the voice that spoke to John will speak to us: *Look, I am making everything new.*

How to Use This Book

This workbook is designed to guide you through a careful and encouraging study of heaven: the eternal home promised to God's people. Each lesson includes clear sections to help you read, reflect, and apply God's word.

1. Read the Passage

Every lesson starts with a key Scripture passage. Take your time to read it slowly, more than once. These passages, especially from Revelation 21–22, are meant to lift your eyes beyond the current world and help you see the certainty of God's promises.

2. From the Text

This section explains the meaning of the passage. It offers the background, context, and main ideas of the verses being studied. Read these notes carefully. They are not just commentary; they are an invitation to think deeply about what God is revealing.

3. Application

Truth always leads to transformation. The application section connects the text to daily life. It will help you see how the promises of heaven shape your priorities, endurance, and faith in the present.

4. For Discussion

Each lesson ends with a few simple questions for group or personal reflection. These are designed to start conversations, cultivate gratitude, and deepen faith. Please don't rush through them. Allow them to open their hearts.

5. Stay Focused on Hope

As you go through this study, keep in mind the main goal: not to satisfy curiosity about heaven's details, but to strengthen your confidence in God's promises. Heaven represents the fulfillment of His grace, the home He has prepared for His children, and the hope that carries us through every season of life.

Take time each week to read, pray, and meditate on what you learn. Let the words of John's vision sink deeply into your heart. The more we focus on the home that awaits us, the more faithfully we will walk toward it.

PART ONE

Our Hope of Heaven

From the beginning, God's people have lived with their eyes fixed on something greater than this world. Abraham looked for a city with foundations, and early Christians professed they were strangers and exiles on the earth. In this section, we will see how the hope of heaven has always guided God's people and how it should shape our lives today.

Looking for a City
Hebrews 11:13–16

These all died in faith, although they had not received the things that were promised. But they saw them from a distance, greeted them, and confessed that they were foreigners and temporary residents on the earth. Now those who say such things make it clear that they are seeking a homeland. If they were thinking about where they came from, they would have had an opportunity to return. But they now desire a better place—a heavenly one. Therefore, God is not ashamed to be called their God, for he has prepared a city for them (Hebrews 11:13–16).

Class Overview: This introductory lesson sets the stage for our study on heaven, and what themes we will cover in the coming weeks. By grounding ourselves in the promises of Scripture, from Abraham's longing for a city with foundations to John's vision of the New Jerusalem, we will see that heaven is not a vague idea but the certain home of God's people. This study will help us lift our eyes above the temporary struggles of life and focus on the eternal promises of God.

Class Objectives:
By the end of this class, you should be able to:
1. Recognize why the study of heaven is relevant for Christians today.
2. Trace how Abraham, the early Christians, and John all looked forward to a heavenly city.
3. Identify the four main themes of the quarter's study: hope, vision, life, and fulfillment.
4. Explain how the promise of heaven motivates holiness, endurance, hope, and mission.
5. Commit to keeping Hebrews 13:14 in mind as the guiding verse for the quarter.

Introduction:
The Big Picture of Heaven

A FEW YEARS AGO, I saw a video of a soldier surprising his family after a long deployment. He had been away for nearly a year. The footage showed his wife and children waiting in the airport terminal, not knowing when he would walk in. Then suddenly, he appeared. His children saw him first. They didn't hesitate; they didn't walk; they ran as fast as they could, threw their arms around his neck, and clung to him. His wife followed, tears flowing down her face. There was laughter, crying, joy, and relief all at once.

That kind of moment is powerful even to witness as an outsider. But imagine what it meant to that family. The waiting, the longing, the counting of days … all fulfilled in one embrace.

And that is just a glimpse of what Scripture describes about heaven. We are waiting, longing, counting the days. Paul says in Philippians 3:20 that *our citizenship is in heaven, and we eagerly wait for a Savior from there, the Lord Jesus Christ.* One day, the waiting will end. One day, faith will become sight. And when that day comes, the joy will far surpass any airport reunion.

When you hear the word *heaven,* what image comes to mind? For many, it's shaped more by popular culture than by Scripture. Cartoons and movies depict clouds, harps, halos, and even floating figures in the sky. For others, heaven feels distant and hazy, almost unreal; something to think about only when life ends.

However, the Bible describes heaven in a very different way. It is not myth or wishful thinking; it is God's promise. It is the *home of the soul,* the eternal city prepared for those who belong to Him. In John 14:2–3, Jesus plainly said: *In my Father's house are many rooms … I am going away to prepare a place for you … I will come again and take you to myself, so that where I am you may be also.* That's not vague. That's personal. That's a promise.

Why does this matter? Because what we believe about the future shapes how we live in the present. Paul wrote in 2 Corinthians 4:16–18 that our momentary suffering is nothing compared to the eternal weight of glory. Abraham was willing to live in tents and wander as a stranger because *he was looking forward to the city that has foundations, whose architect and builder is God* (Hebrews 11:10). And John saw the New Jerusalem descending, where *God's dwelling is with humanity, and he will live with them* (Revelation 21:3).

That's the goal of our study together. To set aside cultural clichés and let God's word paint the picture. To learn not only *what heaven will be like,* but also *how the promise of heaven should shape our daily walk now.*

As we start, consider this: **What do you most long for when you think about heaven?** Is it a reunion with loved ones? Rest from pain? Or seeing God face-to-face? Scripture points us to all these things and more. And every promise is sure because God Himself has spoken.

Why Heaven Matters Now

For many people, heaven feels like a subject for funerals. Something we'll think about *later,* when life is over. But the Bible presents heaven as something that should shape us *now.* Paul wrote in 2 Corinthians 4:16–18: *Therefore, we do not give up. Even though our outer person is being destroyed, our inner person is being renewed day by day. For our momentary light affliction is producing for us an absolutely incomparable eternal weight of glory. So we do not focus on what is seen, but on what is unseen. For what is seen is temporary, but what is unseen is eternal.* Paul was saying the way to endure suffering now is to keep eternity in view. If all we see is this world, pain will crush us. However, if we remember what God has promised, we can persevere.

The same point appears in Philippians 3:20–21: *Our citizenship is in heaven, and we eagerly wait for a Savior from there —the Lord Jesus Christ. He will transform the body of our humble condition into the likeness of his glorious body, by the power that enables him to subject everything to himself.*

That changes our perspective. This world gives us mailing addresses, but heaven gives us our identity. That's where we truly belong. And that is why this study matters now. Heaven isn't just comfort for the dying; it's strength for the living. When we set our hearts on what is eternal, fear loses its grip, grief has hope, and temptation loses its appeal.

Heaven in the Story of God's People

From the very beginning, God's people have lived with an awareness that this world is not their final home.

- **Abraham's Faith**: Hebrews 11:9–10 tells us Abraham lived in tents "like a stranger in a foreign country" because *he was looking forward to the city that has foundations, whose architect and builder is God.* Imagine the contrast: flimsy tents that wear out quickly vs. a city with eternal foundations. Abraham's eyes were set on something permanent, something only God could build.
- **Confession of the Faithful**: Hebrews 11:13–16 says they "confessed that they were foreigners and temporary residents on the earth … they are seeking a homeland … a better place; a heavenly one." That confession wasn't weakness. It was confidence. They admitted they didn't belong here, and because of that, God "is not ashamed to be called their God."
- **The Early Christians**: Hebrews 13:14 repeats the same truth: *For we do not have an enduring city here; instead, we seek the one to come.* The church never saw itself as settled in this world. They were on the move toward something greater.
- **Jesus' Promise**: In John 14:2–3, Jesus told His disciples that He was preparing a place for them and that He would come again to bring them there. The story of God's people is always a story of waiting and trusting, with heaven as the goal.
- **John's Vision**: And near the end of Scripture, Revelation 21:1–4 brings all of this to fulfillment: the New Jerusalem, where God dwells with His people and every tear is wiped away. The tent is being replaced by a city. The wandering is replaced by home.

What We Will Study in This Class

As we move through the next three months, our goal is not just to talk about heaven in the abstract. We are going to open Scripture and let God show us what awaits. The quarter naturally divides into four sections:

- **Our Hope of Heaven**: We'll begin with Abraham, the early Christians, and the longing of God's people for a better country. Their example reminds us that heaven has always been the goal for those who trust God.
- **The Vision of Heaven**: Then we will step into Revelation 21–22 and see the city itself. The beauty, the light, the walls, the gates, the very structure of it all; these images are designed to stir our hope and anchor our faith.
- **Life in the Heavenly City**: Most of our quarter will be spent here, thinking about what makes heaven truly glorious. Joy without end. Privileges beyond what we can imagine. God's unbroken presence. Eternal fellowship. Worship that never grows old.
- **The Fulfillment of Heaven**: Finally, we will close with the promise of rest. Heaven is not only glorious in description; it is final in reality. Perfect peace, eternal communion with God, and rest for His people.

This class isn't about satisfying curiosity or answering every question we might have. It's about fixing our hearts on God's promises. As Titus 1:2 says, we live *in the hope of eternal life that God, who cannot lie, promised before time began.*

How the Hope of Heaven Shapes Us

The Bible never presents heaven just as information. It is always motivation. Knowing where we are headed should change how we live today.

- **Heaven motivates holiness.**
  - Colossians 3:1–4: *So if you have been raised with Christ, seek the things above, where Christ is ... Set your minds on things above, not on earthly things.*

- Because our lives are hidden with Christ in God, we are called to live differently. Every choice now is shaped by where we are headed.
- **Heaven gives endurance in suffering.**
  - Romans 8:18: *For I consider that the sufferings of this present time are not worth comparing with the glory that is going to be revealed to us.*
  - Paul does not deny suffering. He gives us perspective. Heaven outweighs whatever burdens we carry here.
- **Heaven provides hope in death.**
  - 1 Thessalonians 4:13–18: *We do not want you to be uninformed … so that you will not grieve like the rest, who have no hope.*
  - The hope of resurrection and reunion changes the way we face the death of loved ones and our own mortality.
- **Heaven calls us to mission.**
  - If heaven is real, we want others to share in it. Jesus said in Matthew 28:19–20: *Go therefore and make disciples of all nations … teaching them to observe everything I have commanded you.*
  - Evangelism is not just a duty: it is an invitation to eternal joy.

Conclusion

When we discuss heaven, we are not talking about fantasy or wishful thinking. We are referring to God's promises; promises rooted in His word, sealed by the resurrection of Jesus Christ, and assured by the Spirit who dwells in us.

Abraham lived like a stranger because he was seeking a city with foundations. The early Christians faced hardships because they knew *we do not have an enduring city here; instead, we seek the one to come* (Hebrews 13:14). And John, near the end of Scripture, saw that city: radiant, secure, filled with God's presence.

That is our hope. That is our home. And it should change the way we live today. Heaven calls us to holiness, gives us endurance in trials, provides us hope in death, and moves us to invite others along.

As we start this quarter, I want to challenge you: **don't treat heaven as an afterthought. Let it influence how you live this week.** When you're tempted, remember where you belong. When you're weary, remember the rest ahead. When you're discouraged, remember the glory that's coming. *For we do not have an enduring city here; instead, we seek the one to come.* Heaven is not just our future home; it is the promise that shapes how we live today.

For Discussion

1. When you picture heaven, what comes to mind first, and where did that image come from?

   _____

   _____

   _____

2. Why do you think Abraham was willing to live as a stranger in tents while waiting for "a city with foundations" (Hebrews 11:10)?

   _____

   _____

   _____

3. In what ways does remembering that our "citizenship is in heaven" (Philippians 3:20) change how we live here on earth?

   _____

   _____

   _____

4. Which of the four ways heaven shapes us, holiness, endurance, hope, or mission, speaks most to you right now? Why?

   _____

   _____

   _____

5. How can we, as a church, encourage one another to keep our eyes fixed on the city that is to come?

   _____

   _____

   _____

Abraham Looked for a City

Hebrews 11:8–16

By faith, Abraham, when he was called, obeyed and set out for a place that he was going to receive as an inheritance. He went out, even though he did not know where he was going. By faith, he stayed as a foreigner in the land of promise, living in tents as did Isaac and Jacob, coheirs of the same promise. For he was looking forward to the city that has foundations, whose architect and builder is God. By faith, even Sarah herself, when she was unable to have children, received power to conceive offspring, even though she was past the age, since she considered that the one who had promised was faithful. Therefore, from one man—in fact, from one as good as dead—came offspring as numerous as the stars of the sky and as innumerable as the grains of sand along the seashore. These all died in faith, although they had not received the things that were promised. But they saw them from a distance, greeted them, and confessed that they were foreigners and temporary residents on the earth. Now those who say such things make it clear that they are seeking a homeland. If they were thinking about where they came from, they would have had an opportunity to return. But they now desire a better place—a heavenly one. Therefore, God is not ashamed to be called their God, for he has prepared a city for them
(Hebrews 11:8–16).

Class Overview: This lesson explores Abraham's life of faith as described in Hebrews 11:8–16. Though called to an earthly land, Abraham lived as a pilgrim, dwelling in tents while longing for a city with foundations, designed and built by God. His perspective teaches us to see ourselves as strangers and exiles on the earth, pressing forward toward the better country God has prepared. Abraham's example challenges us to obey without all the details, to endure with a heavenly perspective, and to live in hope of God's eternal promises.

Class Objectives:

By the end of this class, you should be able to:

1. Describe Abraham's obedience in leaving his homeland without knowing his destination.
2. Explain how Abraham's tent-dwelling points to the temporary nature of life on earth.
3. Recognize the significance of Abraham looking for a "city with foundations" built by God.
4. Apply the idea of being "strangers and exiles" to the Christian life today.
5. Reflect on how Abraham's hope for a better country motivates our own perseverance in faith.

Introduction:
Abraham Looked for a City

WHEN WE THINK OF ABRAHAM, we often picture the great promises: *I will make you into a great nation ... all the peoples on earth will be blessed through you* (Genesis 12:2–3). But what stands out in Hebrews 11 is not just the promises Abraham received, but how he lived while waiting for them.

God called Abraham to leave his homeland, his family, and everything familiar, and go to a place he had never seen. Hebrews 11:8 says, *By faith Abraham, when he was called, obeyed and set out for a place that he was going to receive as an inheritance. He went out, even though he did not know where he was going.* That one verse summarizes his life: he obeyed without seeing, he trusted without knowing.

And how did he live? Verse 9 tells us he "stayed as a foreigner in the land of promise, living in tents with Isaac and Jacob." Think about that: God promised him a land, but all he owned of it in his lifetime was a cave he bought to bury Sarah. He lived in tents his entire life.

Have you ever moved into a new house and had to live out of boxes for a while? Maybe the furniture wasn't delivered yet, or you were waiting on a closing date, so you couldn't fully unpack. Everything feels temporary. You can function, but it doesn't feel like home. You tell yourself, *This is fine for now, but it's not where I'm settling.*

That's how Abraham lived, not just for a few weeks, but for his whole life. He pitched his tent, moved when God told him, and never really "settled down." Why? Because he knew Canaan wasn't the final home. He was looking for something more permanent: *a city with foundations, whose architect and builder is God* (Hebrews 11:10).

And that's our situation, too. No matter how stable our homes or lives may feel, we are still "living out of boxes" in this world. This is not where we truly settle. Like Abraham, we are waiting for God's city.

Abraham's Obedient Faith
(Hebrews 11:8–9)

The story of Abraham begins with a call. God told him, *Go from your land, your relatives, and your father's house to the land that I will show you* (Genesis 12:1). Hebrews 11:8 reflects on that moment: *By faith, Abraham, when he was called, obeyed and set out for a place that he was going to receive as an inheritance. He went out, even though he did not know where he was going.*

From the Text
1. **Faith obeys even without full details.**
   Abraham left, not knowing where the journey would end. He didn't have a road map, he didn't know the geography, and he had no idea what awaited him. But he trusted the One who called him.
2. **Faith accepts living as a stranger.**
   Verse 9 says, *By faith he stayed as a foreigner in the land of promise, living in tents with Isaac and Jacob, coheirs of the same promise.* Abraham lived in the very land God promised, but as a foreigner, never as an owner. His faith was content with tents, because he trusted the promise of something greater.

Application
- Faith is not just believing; it's moving when God says move.
- Like Abraham, we often must obey without knowing all the details; trusting the character of God more than the clarity of the path.
- Our willingness to live as "foreigners" here shows that we believe this world is not our final home.

Abraham's Heavenly Perspective
(Hebrews 11:10, 13)

Hebrews 11 explains *why* Abraham was willing to live in tents his whole life:

Verse 10: *"For he was looking forward to the city that has foundations, whose architect and builder is God."*

Verse 13: *"These all died in faith, although they had not received the things that were promised. But they saw them from a distance, greeted them, and confessed that they were foreigners and temporary residents on the earth."*

From the Text
1. **Heaven, in contrast with tents:**
   Abraham's tents were temporary. The city of God has foundations—solid, permanent, eternal. Faith allowed him to look past the temporary to the lasting.
2. **He saw promises from a distance.**
   Abraham never saw the whole picture in his lifetime. Yet he "greeted" the promises as though they were already real. That's faith—treating unseen promises as certain.
3. **He embraced being a foreigner.**
   Instead of settling down, Abraham openly admitted he didn't belong here. His very lifestyle was a confession of hope in God's city.

Application
- A heavenly perspective means refusing to treat this life as if it were permanent.
- It means believing God's promises enough to endure, even when we don't see them fulfilled right away.

- It means embracing the identity of a stranger here, not clinging too tightly to this world.

God's Better Country
(Hebrews 11:14–16)

Hebrews 11:14–16 explains what Abraham and the faithful were really seeking:

*"Now those who say such things make it clear that they are seeking
a homeland. If they were thinking about where they came from, they would
have had an opportunity to return. But they now desire a better place—
a heavenly one. Therefore, God is not ashamed to be called their God,
for he has prepared a city for them."*

From the Text
1. **Seeking a Homeland.**
   Abraham could have gone back to Ur, but he didn't. His eyes weren't on the past. His faith pressed him forward. Faith always looks ahead. It refuses to return to its old life.
2. **A Better Place.**
   The "better country" is heaven itself. It is better because it is eternal, because it is perfect, and because it is God's dwelling. Every earthly homeland, no matter how good, eventually disappoints. Heaven will not.
3. **God's Commendation.**
   God is not ashamed to be called their God. Their faith honored Him, and His response was to honor them. He prepared a city for them, and for us. What greater approval could we ever seek than to have God gladly call Himself our God?

Application
- True faith is forward-looking. It does not go back to the old ways, even when things get difficult.
- Our deepest longings for security, belonging, and permanence are fulfilled only in heaven.

- When we live as pilgrims, trusting in God's promises, we bring honor to His name.

Conclusion:
Living Like Abraham

Abraham's life was marked by trust in promises he could not yet see. He left his home without knowing the destination. He lived in tents while waiting for a city with foundations. He embraced life as a stranger because he knew God was preparing a better country.

That's the lesson for us: faith doesn't cling to what is temporary. It steps out in obedience, endures with hope, and keeps its eyes fixed on the eternal. Like Abraham, we live in "tents" now —fragile bodies, unstable circumstances, and passing possessions. But like Abraham, we believe God has prepared something better.

Hebrews 11 reminds us that this way of life honors God: *"God is not ashamed to be called their God, for he has prepared a city for them"* (v. 16). If we keep walking by faith, if we confess with our lives that this world is not our home, then one day we will enter that city: not as strangers, but as citizens.

For Discussion

1. What do you find most striking about Abraham's willingness to obey God without knowing the destination?

   _____

   _____

2. How do Abraham's tents serve as a picture of the temporary nature of our own lives today?

   _____

   _____

3. Hebrews 11:13 says Abraham and others "saw the promises from a distance and greeted them." What does that teach us about faith?

   _____

   _____

4. In what ways are we tempted to "return" to old securities instead of pressing forward like Abraham (v. 15)?

   _____

   _____

5. What does it mean to you personally that *"God is not ashamed to be called their God"* (v. 16)

   _____

   _____

   _____

We Are Looking for a City
Hebrews 13:14

For we do not have an enduring city here; instead, we seek the one to come,
Hebrews 13:14.

Class Overview: This lesson emphasizes the temporary nature of life on earth and the Christian's call to seek the eternal city that God has prepared. Drawing from Hebrews 13:14, we will consider how earthly "cities" and securities inevitably fade, but the city of God endures forever. By learning to live as pilgrims and strangers here, we strengthen our faith, reorient our priorities, and fix our eyes on the city to come.

Class Objectives:
By the end of this class, you should be able to:
1. Explain the meaning of Hebrews 13:14 in its context.
2. Contrast the temporary nature of earthly "cities" with the permanence of God's city.
3. Describe what it means to actively "seek" the city to come.
4. Apply the biblical concept of living as pilgrims and strangers to daily life.
5. Reflect on how the hope of heaven provides strength to endure trials and reorders priorities.

Introduction

ONE OF THE MOST CHALLENGING ASPECTS OF THE CHRISTIAN LIFE is remembering that this world is not our ultimate home. We get settled. We put down roots. We start to measure our security by jobs, houses, routines, or possessions. But Hebrews 13:14 reminds us: *For we do not have an enduring city here; instead, we seek the one to come.*

That statement concludes the letter to the Hebrews, written to Christians who were weary and tempted to return to their old ways. They were pressured by culture, weighed down by persecution, and discouraged by hardships. The writer's answer wasn't to tell them to make this life easier; it was to lift their eyes higher. There is no lasting city here. Nothing on earth will endure. But there is a city to come, and that is where our hope lies.

We know what it's like to want stability. We build cities, systems, and safety nets because we long for permanence. Yet everything here eventually fades … nations rise and fall, economies crash, homes decay, even our bodies wear out. Only the city God has prepared will last.

This lesson invites us to reflect on how we live as people seeking the eternal city. Just as Abraham looked for a city with foundations (Hebrews 11:10), we now confess that our citizenship is not here but in heaven (Philippians 3:20). That perspective shapes our priorities, endurance, and mission.

The Temporary Nature of Earthly Cities

Hebrews 13:14 begins with a straightforward statement: *For we do not have an enduring city here.* Throughout history, people have built cities as symbols of safety, strength, and permanence. But no matter how impressive they seemed, none of them lasted.

Take Babylon, for example. At its peak, Babylon was the most magnificent city in the ancient world. It stood along the Euphrates River with massive double walls so wide that chariots could ride across them. Its gates, like the famous Ishtar Gate, were adorned with brilliant blue tiles depicting lions and dragons. Ancient writers described its hanging gardens as one of the Seven Wonders of the World. Babylon was the center of power, wealth, and learning. It looked invincible.

But its greatness didn't last. Corruption and arrogance weakened it, and God's prophets announced its downfall (Isaiah 13:19–22; Jeremiah

51). In 539 B.C., the Persians diverted the Euphrates River, marched in under the walls, and the city fell overnight. From there, it declined, was abandoned, and eventually became a wasteland. Today, Babylon is nothing but ruins in Iraq; a reminder that even the mightiest "enduring" city of men cannot stand forever.

The same principle applies to our personal lives. We build routines, gather possessions, invest in careers, and imagine stability. Yet all of it is temporary. Homes crumble—health declines. Wealth disappears. As James 4:14 reminds us, *You don't even know what tomorrow will bring—what your life will be! For you are like vapor that appears for a little while, then vanishes.*

This isn't meant to make us despair. It's intended to reset our expectations. If we are looking for lasting security here, we will always be disappointed. Earthly "cities" cannot endure. Only God's city is eternal.

Application:
- Don't cling too tightly to what cannot last.
- Recognize that disappointment often comes when we expect permanence from temporary things.
- Let the passing nature of this world push you to long more deeply for the world to come.

Seeking the City to Come

Hebrews 13:14 doesn't just tell us what we *don't* have —i.e., an enduring city here —it also tells us what we *do* have: *we seek the one to come.*

From the Text
1. **Seeking implies pursuit.**
   The Greek word suggests a steady searching, longing, and striving after. It's not passive; it's active. We are not just *waiting* for heaven; we are *seeking* it. Colossians 3:1–2 says, *So if you have been raised with Christ, seek the things above, where Christ is … Set your minds on things above, not on earthly things.*

2. **The city is in the future, but certain.**
   Hebrews 12:22–23 already calls us citizens of the heavenly
   Jerusalem. In one sense, we belong there now. In another sense, we
   are still on the way. Like Abraham, we confess we are strangers here
   because our true home is still ahead.
3. **Seeking changes in priorities.**
   If we are seeking the city to come, we will invest in what lasts: God's
   word, God's people, and God's mission. Jesus said, *But store up for*
   yourselves treasures in heaven … For where your treasure is, there your
   heart will be also (Matthew 6:20–21).

Application:

- Seeking heaven means orienting our lives toward eternity, not
  just drifting along with the present.
- It challenges us to evaluate our choices: Am I living like my
  citizenship is here—or there?
- Seeking heaven doesn't make us useless here; it makes us
  faithful, because we know what really matters.

Living as Pilgrims

Seeking the city to come means accepting the reality that we are *not at*
home here. Scripture often uses the language of pilgrimage to describe
the Christian life.

1. **Hebrews 11:13–16** reminds us that Abraham and the faithful
   "confessed that they were foreigners and temporary residents on the
   earth." They admitted they didn't belong here, and God honored
   them for it.
2. **1 Peter 2:11** calls believers "strangers and exiles" and urges us to
   abstain from sinful desires that wage war against the soul. Peter's
   point: live differently, because you belong somewhere else.
3. **Philippians 3:20** says our citizenship is in heaven. Whatever earthly
   passport we carry, our identity is tied to Christ.

What does this mean for us?

1. **Pilgrims travel light.**
   Pilgrims don't put down permanent roots. They hold possessions loosely because they know they're temporary.
2. **Pilgrims endure hardship.**
   The journey isn't always easy, but the destination is worth it.
3. **Pilgrims live with direction.**
   They don't wander. Instead, they keep their eyes fixed on the city that lies ahead.

Application:

- Living as pilgrims reshapes our daily priorities. We live holy lives, endure trials, and keep moving forward because heaven is our goal.
- It also reshapes our witness. When others see us living differently — refusing to cling too tightly to this world — they see evidence of our hope in Christ.

Conclusion:
Fixing Our Eyes on the City to Come

Hebrews 13:14 is both a warning and a promise.

- The warning: *We do not have an enduring city here.* Nothing in this world lasts. Every city, every system, every possession eventually fades.
- The promise: *Instead, we seek the one to come.* There is a city that will endure, built by God Himself, prepared for His people.

Like Abraham, we live in tents. Like the early Christians, we are strangers and exiles here. But our eyes are set on something better: a homeland, a heavenly city where God dwells with His people forever. That hope gives us strength to endure, courage to obey, and direction for our lives today.

So don't settle for less. Don't treat what is temporary as permanent. Instead, live as pilgrims who keep moving forward. We are not home yet … but one day, we will be.

For Discussion

1. Why do we often treat earthly things as if they will last forever, even when Scripture says they won't?

   _____

   _____

2. How does the fall of great cities like Babylon remind us of the truth in Hebrews 13:14?

   _____

   _____

3. What does it practically mean to "seek the city to come" in your daily life?

   _____

   _____

4. How can living as strangers and pilgrims shape how we handle possessions, struggles, and relationships?

   _____

   _____

5. What specific changes might you need to make to live more like a pilgrim on the way to God's city?

   _____

   _____

   _____

PART TWO

The Vision of Heaven

Now, we will turn to John's vision in Revelation 21–22, where God pulls back the curtain and shows His people the glory of their eternal home. These lessons highlight the holy city, the New Jerusalem, descending from heaven, radiant with God's glory and prepared like a bride. We will explore its beauty, size, and structure—images meant not to satisfy human curiosity but to inspire faith and hope. The contrast between the fallen cities of men and the eternal city of God reminds us that heaven is secure, glorious, and certain. By fixing our eyes on this vision, we strengthen our endurance and renew our longing for the city that is to come.

John's Vision of the Heavenly City

Revelation 21–22

Then I saw a new heaven and a new earth; for the first heaven and the first earth had passed away, and the sea was no more. I also saw the holy city, the new Jerusalem, coming down out of heaven from God, prepared like a bride adorned for her husband. Then I heard a loud voice from the throne: Look, God's dwelling is with humanity, and he will live with them. They will be his peoples, and God himself will be with them and will be their God. He will wipe away every tear from their eyes. Death will be no more; grief, crying, and pain will be no more, because the previous things have passed away (Revelation 21:1–4).

Class Overview: In this lesson, we will study John's breathtaking vision of the New Jerusalem. After the fall of Babylon and the defeat of evil, God reveals the holy city coming down from heaven, radiant with His glory and prepared like a bride for Christ. Revelation 21–22 paints a picture of a new creation, God's permanent dwelling with His people, the end of sorrow and death, and a city of unmatched beauty. This vision assures us that heaven is real, certain, and far greater than anything we can imagine.

Class Objectives:
By the end of this class, you should be able to:
1. Explain the meaning of a "new heaven and new earth" in Revelation 21:1–2.
2. Describe the significance of God dwelling permanently with His people.
3. Identify the promises of no more death, grief, crying, or pain.
4. Interpret the imagery of beauty, radiance, and perfection in the New Jerusalem.

5. Apply this vision as a source of hope and encouragement in daily life.

Introduction

NEAR THE END OF SCRIPTURE, AFTER BABYLON'S FALL AND EVIL'S DEFEAT, John is shown a breathtaking vision: the New Jerusalem descending from heaven by God (Revelation 21–22). If Abraham longed for a city with foundations, and if we are searching for the city to come, John reveals what that city looks like.

Revelation 21:1–4 appears at the end of the Bible for a reason. The story of Scripture doesn't conclude with judgment, war, or destruction. It concludes with a homecoming: the marriage of the Lamb and His bride, God dwelling with His people, and the end of everything that causes sorrow.

For Christians who were weary, persecuted, or afraid, this vision served as an anchor. And it continues to do so for us. When life feels uncertain and the world feels dark, we turn to the last pages of Scripture and remember this is how the story ends.

The New Creation:
A New Heaven and a New Earth

John begins his vision in Revelation 21:1–2: *Then I saw a new heaven and a new earth; for the first heaven and the first earth had passed away, and the sea was no more. I also saw the holy city, the new Jerusalem, coming down out of heaven from God, prepared like a bride adorned for her husband.*

From the Text
1. **A new heaven and a new earth.**
   The old order, marked by sin, corruption, and death, is gone. Isaiah 65:17 had promised: *For I will create new heavens and a new earth; the past events will not be remembered or come to mind.* This is not a

patchwork repair of the old creation but God's complete renewal.

2. **The sea was no more.**
   In biblical imagery, the sea often represents chaos, danger, and separation (Psalm 46:2–3; Revelation 13:1). The removal of the sea symbolizes the end of all that threatens God's people.

3. **The holy city, the new Jerusalem.**
   Unlike Babel or Babylon, which man tried to build, this city comes *down from God*. It is described as a bride, beautiful and prepared for her husband, pointing to purity, joy, and an intimate relationship.

Application

- The hope of heaven is not just escape from this world … it is renewal. God is making all things new.
- Chaos, danger, and separation will be gone forever.
- Heaven is not a human achievement but God's gift, prepared like a bride for His people.

God's Dwelling with His People

Revelation 21:3–4 continues John's vision: *Then I heard a loud voice from the throne: Look, God's dwelling is with humanity, and he will live with them. They will be his peoples, and God himself will be with them and will be their God. He will wipe away every tear from their eyes. Death will be no more; grief, crying, and pain will be no more, because the previous things have passed away.*

From the Text

1. **God's dwelling is with humanity.**
   The word "dwelling" (Greek *skēnē*) echoes the tabernacle in the wilderness, where God's presence was among His people (Exodus 25:8). In heaven, there will be no separation, no veil, no temple needed; God Himself will live with His people permanently.

2. **They will be His people**.
   This is the covenant promise fulfilled. Repeated throughout Scripture (Leviticus 26:11–12; Jeremiah 31:33), it now reaches its ultimate completion. What Israel anticipated in shadows becomes

full reality in eternity.

3. **The end of sorrow.**
God personally wipes away every tear. Death, grief, crying, and pain, all the things that have marked human existence since the fall, are forever gone. This is not just relief from suffering; it is the complete reversal of the curse.

Application

- The greatest blessing of heaven is not golden streets or pearly gates: it is God's presence.
- The end of sorrow gives us endurance now. Romans 8:18: *For I consider that the sufferings of this present time are not worth comparing with the glory that is going to be revealed to us.*
- Our hope is not just survival, but joy: the joy of being fully at home with God.

The Glory of the New Jerusalem

Revelation 21:9–11, 18–21 gives us a glimpse of heaven's beauty: *Then one of the seven angels … spoke with me: 'Come, I will show you the bride, the wife of the Lamb.' He then carried me away in the Spirit to a great, high mountain and showed me the holy city, Jerusalem, coming down out of heaven from God, arrayed with God's glory. Her radiance was like a precious jewel, like a jasper stone, clear as crystal … The building material of its wall was jasper, and the city was pure gold, transparent as glass. The foundations of the city wall were adorned with every kind of jewel … The twelve gates are twelve pearls; each gate was made of a single pearl. The main street of the city was pure gold, transparent as glass.*

From the Text

1. **The city as a bride.**
The angel calls the city "the bride, the wife of the Lamb." The New Jerusalem represents not only a place but also God's people: redeemed, purified, and joined to Christ forever.

2. **The radiance of glory.**
The city shines with God's glory, like precious jewels reflecting light.

This is not about earthly wealth: it's about brilliance, beauty, and holiness.

3. **Imagery of perfection.**
   Streets of transparent gold, walls of jasper, gates of pearl—all symbolize unmatched beauty, purity, and permanence. These images remind us: nothing man has built, no matter how impressive, compares with what God has prepared.

Application

- Heaven is described in terms of beauty to stir our longing and lift our imagination.
- These images remind us that heaven's glory comes from God Himself—not from the materials, but from His presence.
- If God prepared something this glorious for His people, we can endure whatever trials we face now with hope.

Conclusion

John's vision concludes with hope as the Bible closes. The old order has passed away, and God reveals a new heaven and a new earth. The holy city descends, shining with glory, prepared like a bride for her husband. God Himself dwells with His people, wiping away every tear and forever removing death, sorrow, and pain. The New Jerusalem shines with unimaginable beauty, reflecting the glory of the One who resides there.

This vision isn't intended to satisfy curiosity but to build faith. For weary Christians, it reminds us that this world isn't our home. For suffering Christians, it assures us that the pain won't last. For all of us, it calls us to keep seeking the city's coming.

For Discussion

1. What does John's description of a "new heaven and new earth" teach us about God's plan for creation?

    _____

    _____

2. Why is God's presence with His people the greatest blessing of heaven?

    _____

    _____

3. Which of the promises in Revelation 21:4—no more tears, death, grief, or pain—speaks most powerfully to you today?

    _____

    _____

4. Why do you think Scripture uses imagery of gold, jewels, and pearls to describe heaven?

    _____

    _____

5. How can this vision of the New Jerusalem strengthen your endurance and hope right now?

    _____

    _____

    _____

Heaven: God's Finished Work

Revelation 21:5–8

Then the one seated on the throne said, 'Look, I am making everything new.'
He also said, 'Write, because these words are faithful and true.' Then he said
to me, 'It is done! I am the Alpha and the Omega, the beginning and the end.
I will freely give to the thirsty from the spring of the water of life. The one
who conquers will inherit these things, and I will be his God, and he will be
my son. But the cowards, faithless, detestable, murderers, sexually immoral,
sorcerers, idolaters, and all liars —their share will be in the lake that burns
with fire and sulfur, which is the second death', (Revelation 21:5–8).

Class Overview: Heaven is the completion of all God's work in redemption. In this brief but powerful section, God Himself speaks, declaring the end of sin, the fulfillment of His promises, and the beginning of eternal life for His people. The same voice that spoke creation into being now proclaims, "It is done." Every wound healed, every tear wiped away, every promise kept. Heaven is not an escape; it is God's finished masterpiece.

Class Objectives:
By the end of this class, you should be able to:
1. Explain the meaning of God's statement, "I am making everything new."
2. Understand the significance of the words, "It is done."
3. Identify the contrast between the overcomer and the unbelieving.
4. Recognize heaven as the final stage of God's redemptive plan.
5. Apply this hope to daily endurance and faithfulness.

Introduction

EVERY STORY HAS A MOMENT WHEN EVERYTHING COMES TOGETHER. The loose ends are tied, the conflicts resolved, and the purpose finally clear. Revelation 21:5–8 is that moment in the story of God. After all the struggle, suffering, and waiting, the One who sits on the throne speaks—and His first words are, *Look, I am making everything new.*

This isn't the tired optimism of a broken world trying to fix itself. It's the voice of the Creator who spoke the universe into existence, now announcing the completion of His eternal plan. Everything that sin ruined, every tear, every scar, every grave, has been undone by His power. What began in Genesis as a world spoiled by rebellion now ends in Revelation as a world restored in righteousness.

John hears God declare, *It is done!* These words carry the same authority as Jesus' cry from the cross: *"It is finished."* At Calvary, redemption was purchased. In Revelation 21, redemption is perfected. The cross began what heaven completes, the full restoration of creation and the eternal fellowship of God and His people.

The words that follow offer both comfort and warning. To the thirsty, God gives freely from the water of life. To the faithful conqueror, He promises inheritance and sonship. But to those who reject Him, only separation and judgment remain. Heaven is not just the end of history; it is the unveiling of God's completed work, where His justice, mercy, and faithfulness stand fully.

When we read this passage, we are invited to marvel at the masterpiece God has been creating since the beginning of time. Every act of grace, every answered prayer, every trial endured, and every soul redeemed points to this moment. Heaven is the ultimate proof that God keeps His word. It is His finished work—perfect, holy, and eternal.

"I Am Making Everything New" (21:5)

Then the one seated on the throne said, 'Look, I am making everything new.' He also said, 'Write, because these words are faithful and true,' (Revelation 21:5).

From the Text

1. **God Himself speaks.**
   This is one of the rare places in Revelation where God directly addresses John. His words come from the throne, the center of authority and holiness. The same power that created the world now announces its renewal.

2. **"I am making everything new."**
   This is not the idea of simply repairing what was broken. The Greek phrase suggests continuous action: "I am in the process of making all things new." God's renewal begins now in His people and will reach full completion in eternity.

3. **Faithful and true.**
   John is told to write these words down because they are trustworthy. They are not wishful hopes or symbolic ideals; they are divine certainties. What God promises, He performs.

4. **Old things have passed away.**
   The old order, sin, death, sorrow, and decay, is gone. Isaiah 65:17 anticipated this: *For I will create new heavens and a new earth; the past events will not be remembered or come to mind.* The former world fades away, replaced by one untouched by sin or time.

Application

God's promise to "make everything new" means that nothing broken will remain broken. Every wrong will be set right, every scar healed, every injustice answered.

- The same God who renews the universe is already renewing us. Paul writes, *If anyone is in Christ, he is a new creation; the old has passed away, and see, the new has come* (2 Corinthians 5:17). Heaven is the completion of that work.

- These words bring assurance to weary hearts. The God who began a good work in us (Philippians 1:6) will finish it. The new creation is not just coming; it has already started in every Christian transformed by His grace.
- When we see decay, pain, or evil in this world, we remember: this is not the final chapter. The throne still stands. The One who sits upon it is making everything new.

"It is Done" (21:6a)

Then he said to me, 'It is done! I am the Alpha and the Omega, the beginning and the end," (Revelation 21:6a).

From the Text
1. **The voice of finality.**
   God's declaration, *It is done,* marks the completion of His redemptive plan. The same God who began creation in Genesis now announces its fulfillment in Revelation. Nothing remains unfinished, nothing uncertain. Every promise has reached its end.
2. **Echo of the cross.**
   These words mirror Jesus' final cry from the cross: "*It is finished*" (John 19:30). At Calvary, redemption was purchased. In heaven, it is perfected. The first statement completed salvation's payment; the second completes its purpose.
3. **The Alpha and the Omega.**
   God identifies Himself as the first and last letters of the Greek alphabet —the beginning and the end. This title shows His sovereignty over all history. What He starts, He sustains. What He promises, He fulfills. From creation to consummation, everything begins and ends with Him.
4. **The end of the story, not the end of life.**
   When God says, "It is done," He does not mean existence ceases. He means the story of redemption has reached its climax. Sin's curse is broken. Evil is defeated. The work of grace stands complete forever.

Application

- These words remind us that our faith is not built on uncertainty. God has already written the ending, and it ends in victory. Our future is not fragile; it is finished.
- When life feels chaotic or incomplete, we can rest in the fact that God is not improvising. The One who began our story has already finished it in His plan.
- Every hardship we endure is part of a larger work God is bringing to completion. We live between two finished statements: "It is finished" at the cross and "It is done" at the throne. Both remind us that the outcome of faith is certain.
- Heaven is not God's last attempt; it is His completed masterpiece. The universe that began with "Let there be light" concludes with "It is done," a world forever filled with that light.

"I Will Freely Give to the Thirsty" (21:6b)

I will freely give to the thirsty from the spring of the water of life, (Revelation 21:6b).

From the Text

1. **The invitation of grace.**
   After declaring His finished work, God extends an open invitation. The word *freely* emphasizes that heaven's blessings are not earned; they are gifts. Grace, from beginning to end, defines God's dealings with humanity.

2. **Thirst speaks to deep longing.**
   Physical thirst is one of the most urgent human needs. Spiritually, it describes the soul's longing for satisfaction and peace. Jesus used the same language in John 7:37–38: *If anyone is thirsty, let him come to me and drink.* Heaven is the final answer to that invitation.

3. **The spring of the water of life.**
   This image recalls the river flowing from God's throne in Revelation 22:1–2. It represents eternal life, refreshment, and unbroken fellowship with God. Isaiah 55:1: *"Come, everyone who is thirsty, come*

to the water." What Isaiah promised, and Jesus offered, God now provides forever.

4. **God as the source.**
The water flows from His throne. It cannot be found in the world, earned through effort, or purchased by wealth. All true life, joy, and peace come directly from Him.

Application

- This verse reminds us that heaven is not a reward for the strong; it is a gift for the thirsty. It is not for the self-sufficient but for those who know their need.
- Even now, this promise applies. The Christian life begins with thirst. Every time we come to God in prayer, worship, or repentance, He refreshes us with living water.
- The generosity of God never runs dry. The same grace that saved us will sustain us through eternity. The spring that begins in Christ will flow without end in heaven.
- The invitation still stands. The Spirit and the Bride say, *"Come!"* (Revelation 22:17). Until the day the water of life flows before us, our mission is to share that invitation with others who are still thirsty.

The One Who Conquers (21:7–8)

The one who conquers will inherit these things, and I will be his God, and he will be my son. But the cowards, faithless, detestable, murderers, sexually immoral, sorcerers, idolaters, and all liars—their share will be in the lake that burns with fire and sulfur, which is the second death, (Revelation 21:7–8).

From the Text

1. **The promise to the conqueror.**
The phrase "the one who conquers" runs throughout Revelation (see 2:7, 11, 17, 26; 3:5, 12, 21). It refers not to those who win earthly battles, but to believers who remain faithful to Christ through trial and temptation. The victory is spiritual endurance.

2. **Inheritance language.**
   "He will inherit these things." Heaven is not a wage earned but an inheritance received. It belongs to those who are children of God. Galatians 4:7 reminds us, *You are no longer a slave but a son, and if a son, then God has made you an heir.* In eternity, the Father gives His faithful children their full inheritance.
3. **"I will be his God, and he will be my son."**
   This is the ultimate covenant promise: God's relationship with His people reaches perfect fulfillment. What was shadowed in the Old Testament (Exodus 6:7; Jeremiah 31:33) is now complete: God and His children living together forever in perfect harmony.
4. **A sobering contrast.**
   Verse 8 stands as a solemn warning. Those who reject God through unbelief, rebellion, or unrepentant sin will face the "second death," eternal separation from Him. Heaven and hell are both real. Grace is free, but it must be received through faith and obedience.

Application

- The Christian life is a battle of endurance. To conquer is to keep faith when the world falls apart. Heaven belongs to those who do not give up.
- The word "inherit" teaches us that salvation is relational. Our reward is not a possession but a Person: God Himself. "I will be his God, and he will be my son." This is the heart of heaven.
- The warning of verse 8 reminds us that choices matter. Faith leads to life; unbelief leads to loss. The same God who promises reward also speaks truth about judgment.
- Perseverance is not about perfection but persistence, refusing to let go of faith. Every act of faithfulness now prepares us for that eternal inheritance.
- When you feel weary or tempted to quit, remember what's waiting. The overcomer doesn't win by strength but by steadfast trust in the One who already conquered death.

Conclusion

Heaven is not a dream or a wish...it is the completion of everything God has been doing since creation. In Revelation 21:5–8, the voice from the throne leaves no doubt: the story is finished, and God's purpose has prevailed. What began with *Let there be light* ends with *It is done*. Every promise He made has been kept. Every wound sin caused has been healed. Every longing of the faithful heart has been satisfied. The Creator who once made all things out of nothing now makes all things new, never to fade or fail again.

For those who thirst, there is living water: freely given, overflowing, and eternal. For those who endure, there is inheritance and belonging. *I will be his God, and he will be my son.* Heaven is not a reward for the strong; it is the home of the faithful.

But this passage also reminds us that not everyone will enter that city. The same God who welcomes the thirsty warns the unbelieving. Heaven's doors are open to all who come through Christ, yet its holiness excludes all that refuses His grace.

When we see the world's brokenness, we can find comfort in the fact that God's work is not yet finished—but it soon will be. And when it is, the voice that spoke to John will speak to us: *It is done.* Until that day, we live as people who trust His promise, drink deeply from His grace, and keep moving forward toward the city He has prepared.

For Discussion

1. When you hear God say, *"I am making everything new,"* what does that promise mean for your life right now?

   _____

   _____

2. How does the statement *It is done* deepen your understanding of God's control over history and your personal spiritual growth?

   _____

   _____

3. Why do you think God uses the image of thirst to describe those who come to Him? How does this shape our invitation to others today?

   _____

   _____

4. What does it mean to "conquer" in everyday Christian life? How can we hold fast when faith feels difficult?

   _____

   _____

5. Which part of God's "finished work" fills you with the most hope: the promise of renewal, the inheritance of sonship, or the assurance of His presence, and why?

   _____

   _____

   _____

The Incredible Size and Structure of the Heavenly City

Revelation 21:15–21

The one who spoke with me had a golden measuring rod to measure the city, its gates, and its wall. The city is laid out in a square; its length and width are the same. He measured the city with the rod at 12,000 stadia. Its length, width, and height are equal. Then he measured its wall, 144 cubits by human measurement, which the angel used (Revelation 21:15–17).

Class Overview: In Revelation 21, John describes the heavenly city with meticulous detail: its massive dimensions, perfect symmetry, dazzling gates, sturdy foundations, and streets paved with pure gold. These features are not meant to provide us with a blueprint, but rather to remind us of heaven's sufficiency, security, and glory. The city is vast enough for all of God's people, strong enough to keep them safe forever, and beautiful enough to reflect His majesty. The design shows that the whole city is the dwelling place of God, where His people will live in His presence for eternity.

Class Objectives:
By the end of this class, you should be able to:
1. To understand the meaning behind the city's immense size and perfect symmetry.
2. To see how the gates and foundations symbolize unity between God's people of all ages.
3. To appreciate the materials of the city as symbols of purity, holiness, and eternal value.
4. To recognize that heaven's structure points to God's presence and eternal security.
5. To deepen our hope and longing for heaven by reflecting on the glory of God displayed in His eternal city.

Introduction

When John is carried away in the Spirit to see the holy city, he witnesses something beyond imagination. Revelation 21 tells us the angel used a gold measuring rod to measure the city, its wall, and its gates. What he recorded exceeds human scale. The city is arranged as a perfect square: its length, width, and height are all equal. Each side measures 12,000 stadia, approximately 1,400 miles. The wall itself is 144 cubits thick. Even the gates and foundations are described in detail, crafted with precious stones and metals of incredible beauty.

Why would God give such specific measurements? It's not just about impressing us with the size. The picture is intended to convey something about the perfection, security, and glory of our eternal home. The city isn't cramped or limited. It's vast, capable of holding the redeemed from all ages. Its perfect symmetry shows the harmony and order of God's eternal plan. And its walls, foundations, and gates demonstrate that nothing sinful will ever enter there.

As we examine the size and structure of the heavenly city, we must remember this: the details are not provided to satisfy our curiosity but to strengthen our faith and deepen our longing. Heaven is a place prepared by God. It is large enough, strong enough, and glorious enough for every soul who belongs to Him.

The Vast Measurements of the City (21:15–17)

The one who spoke with me had a golden measuring rod to measure the city, its gates, and its wall. The city is laid out in a square; its length and width are the same. He measured the city with the rod at 12,000 stadia. Its length, width, and height are equal. Then he measured its wall, 144 cubits by human measurement, which the angel used (Revelation 21:15–17).

From the Text

1. A City Beyond Comprehension.

The angel's golden rod shows the importance of precision. This city is not imagined but carefully measured by God Himself. 12,000 stadia equal about 1,400 miles. That means the city would stretch farther than New York to Dallas or Miami to Denver. And it is just as high as it is wide. If mapped over the United States, the city would cover nearly half the country. The picture is meant to overwhelm us. John is giving us a sense of size that words can hardly contain.

2. **A City of Perfection.**

   The city is a perfect cube. In Scripture, the only other cube was the **Most Holy Place** in the tabernacle and temple (1 Kings 6:20). The Most Holy Place was where God's presence dwelt and where only the high priest could enter once a year. Now, the whole city is the Holy of Holies. God's presence fills it, and His people live in that presence forever. The symmetry of the measurements speaks to God's perfect design. Nothing is crooked, out of balance, or incomplete.

3. **A City of Security.**

   The wall measures 144 cubits thick (about 200 feet). That's thicker than the widest castle walls built in human history. The number "144" (12 x 12) points again to God's people. The wall exists for them, ensuring that what belongs to God will never be threatened again. Evil and sin, which plagued the old world, will never breach these walls. The redeemed will dwell in perfect safety.

Application

- The city's size reminds us that heaven is not small or exclusive. It has been prepared for *all* who obey the gospel. There is room for Abraham, Moses, David, Paul, and you.
- The perfection of the city tells us heaven will not disappoint. Every detail of God's plan is flawless.
- The security of the city assures us of eternal rest. Once we enter, nothing can drive us out.

The Gates and Foundations of the City
(21:12–14; 18–21)

It had a massive high wall with twelve gates; twelve angels were at the gates. The names of the twelve tribes of Israel were inscribed on the gates... The wall of the city had twelve foundations, and the twelve names of the twelve apostles of the Lamb were on the foundations, Revelation 21:12–14.

From the Text

1. **The Twelve Gates.**

   The city has twelve gates, each with twelve angels. The names of the twelve tribes of Israel are written on them (v. 12). Gates are arranged, three on each side, signifying full access from every direction of the earth. Each gate is made from a single pearl (v. 21), symbolizing both purity and great cost. Pearls in Scripture often picture something precious and treasured (cf. Matthew 13:45–46). The gates remind us that heaven is entered only through the Lamb. There is no other way in (John 10:9).

2. **The Twelve Foundations.**

   The city wall rests on twelve foundations (v. 14). Each foundation is inscribed with the names of the twelve apostles of the Lamb. The foundations are decorated with every kind of precious stone (vv. 19–20): jasper, sapphire, emerald, amethyst, and others, showing dazzling variety and beauty. This imagery ties the New Testament apostles with the Old Testament tribes. Together, they show the unity of God's people across all time.

3. **The Significance.**

   The gates and foundations symbolize continuity and completeness; the redeemed are one people, built on the testimony of Israel and the teaching of the apostles. Gates show welcome and access; foundations show strength and stability. The building materials remind us of the surpassing worth of the church and the cost of our salvation.

Application

- The way into heaven is open, but only through Christ.
- God's people are not divided; Old Covenant and New Covenant believers are united in Him.
- Heaven's structure testifies that our faith is not fragile; it rests on an unshakable foundation.

The Materials and Streets of the City (21:18, 21)

The building material of its wall was jasper, and the city was pure gold, transparent as glass. The twelve gates are twelve pearls; each individual gate was made of a single pearl. The main street of the city was pure gold, transparent as glass (Revelation 21:18, 21).

From the Text

1. **Walls and City of Pure Materials.**
   The walls are built of jasper (v. 18), a stone that shines with clear brilliance. It symbolizes purity and God's glory. The entire city is of pure gold, transparent as glass (v. 18). This is not ordinary gold; it is transparent, surpassing anything known on earth. It represents holiness and perfection.

2. **The Gates of Pearl.**
   Each gate is a single pearl (v. 21). Imagine the size of such pearls... far beyond anything earthly. Pearls are formed through suffering; an oyster produces a pearl when wounded. Many see this as a reminder that our entrance into heaven came through the suffering of Christ. The gates show that the way into the city was costly, yet beautiful.

3. **The Street of Gold.**
   The city has a main street of pure gold, transparent as glass (v. 21). Streets in earthly cities show where people walk and live. In heaven, even the streets shine with holiness. Nothing common or corrupt is found there. The beauty is not just for display. It reflects the glory of God and the purity of life within the city.

Application

- The heavenly city is not built with ordinary materials. Its glory is beyond comparison, showing us that heaven is not like this world.
- What men value most (gold, pearls, jewels) are common building materials in heaven. Earth's treasures are nothing compared to the riches of God's eternal dwelling.
- The purity and brilliance of these materials remind us that heaven is a place of holiness, where nothing impure can ever enter.

The Perfect Symmetry and Order of the City (21:16)

The city is laid out in a square; its length and width are the same. He measured the city with the rod at 12,000 stadia. Its length, width, and height are equal (Revelation 21:16).

From the Text

1. **The City as a Perfect Cube.**
   John says, *Its length, width, and height are equal.* This is not random. In Scripture, only one other structure had this shape: the Most Holy Place (1 Kings 6:20). The cube design signals perfection, holiness, and God's presence filling all. The entire city is God's dwelling place.

2. **A Symbol of Completeness.**
   The cube is balanced on all sides: no part lacking, no imperfection. This reflects God's eternal order. In heaven, there is no chaos, disorder, or imbalance. Everything is whole and complete. Unlike earthly cities, which are filled with brokenness, heaven is flawless in every way.

3. **A Dwelling Place for God's People.**
   In the Old Testament, only the high priest entered the Holy of Holies, and only once a year. In the heavenly city, *all God's people* will dwell in His presence forever. There are no limits, no restrictions, no veil. The design shows the fulfillment of God's promise: *"Look, God's dwelling is with humanity, and he will live with them"* (Revelation 21:3).

Application

- The city's structure assures us that heaven is a place of perfect balance and harmony. Nothing will ever be out of place.
- The cube design reminds us that our relationship with God will be complete. We will see Him face to face.
- The order of the city shows us the difference between this world of disorder and the eternal home where all is right.

The Glory Reflected in the City's Structure (21:11, 22–23)

Her radiance was like a precious jewel, like a jasper stone, clear as crystal. I did not see a temple in it, because the Lord God the Almighty and the Lamb are its temple. The city does not need the sun or the moon to shine on it, because the glory of God illuminates it, and its lamp is the Lamb (Revelation 22:11, 22–23).

From the Text

1. **The Radiance of God's Glory.**
   John says the city "shone with the glory of God, like a precious jewel, clear as crystal" (v. 11). The design, materials, and measurements all reflect God's presence. The city itself becomes a mirror of His majesty.

2. **No Temple, No Sun, No Moon.**
   The city has no temple, because the Lord God Almighty and the Lamb are its temple (v. 22). It does not need the sun or the moon. The glory of God gives it light, and the Lamb is its lamp (v. 23). Everything in the city draws attention to God and His Son.

3. **Structure with a Purpose.**
   The walls, gates, foundations, and streets are not random details. They form a city that exists for one reason: to display God's glory and provide a dwelling place for His people. The very design tells us heaven is not about us, it is about Him.

Application

- The glory of heaven is not measured in size, walls, or gold—but in the presence of God Himself.
- The structure reminds us that worship will be our joy and focus for eternity.
- If God is not your glory here, you will not enjoy the glory of His presence there.

Conclusion

When John saw the holy city, its size and structure overwhelmed him. The vast measurements showed that this was a place with room for all God's people. The gates and foundations signified access and stability, built on the testimony of Israel and the apostles. The materials—gold, pearls, precious stones—reminded him that heaven is far wealthier than anything on earth. It's perfect symmetry indicated that this is no ordinary city but the dwelling place of God Himself. And its brilliance revealed that the city is all about His glory.

These descriptions aren't meant to satisfy curiosity or serve as a blueprint. They aim to inspire hope, strengthen faith, and deepen longing. Heaven is real. Heaven is prepared. And heaven is enough. Its size demonstrates its sufficiency. The walls show their safety. Its beauty reveals its perfection. And its glory highlights its purpose—to live forever in God's presence and with the Lamb.

The question we face is straightforward: are we preparing to live there? The gates are open, but only for those who belong to Christ. If this is the city we desire, then let us live now as citizens of heaven, ready for the day when faith turns to sight.

For Discussion

1. What is the significance of the city's perfect cube shape (Revelation 21:16)?
2. How do the twelve gates and twelve foundations show the unity of God's people?
3. What do the precious materials (gold, pearls, stones) teach us about heaven's glory compared to earthly wealth?
4. Why is there no temple in the city, and what does it mean that the Lamb is its lamp?
5. Which detail of the city's description gives you the most hope, and why?

Part Three

Life in the Heavenly City

Now, we will explore what makes heaven truly glorious—not only its beauty but the life we will share there. John describes heaven as a place of complete joy, unimaginable privileges, unending light, and the constant presence of God. It is the eternal fellowship of believers and the unbroken worship of the Lord. These lessons remind us that heaven is more than a destination; it is the fulfillment of every longing of the soul. By considering the blessings of life in the city, we learn to live now with anticipation, holiness, and hope, knowing that the best is yet to come.

All Inclusive Happiness

John 16:22; Revelation 21:3–4

So you also have sorrow now. But I will see you again. Your hearts will rejoice, and no one will take away your joy from you, John 16:22.

Look, God's dwelling is with humanity, and He will live with them. They will be His peoples, and God Himself will be with them and will be their God. He will wipe away every tear from their eyes. Death will be no more; grief, crying, and pain will be no more, because the previous things have passed away, Revelation 21:3–4.

Class Overview: In this lesson, we see heaven as the place of complete and lasting joy. Unlike the fragile happiness of this life, heaven offers an all-inclusive happiness where every sorrow is removed, God's presence is fully realized, eternal life secures our joy forever, and fellowship with the redeemed is perfect. The vision of Revelation 21–22 reminds us that in heaven, nothing will be missing. Every longing of the soul will be satisfied, and every child of God will share in joy that can never be taken away.

Class Objectives:
By the end of this class, you should be able to:
1. Explain why earthly happiness is temporary and incomplete.
2. Identify how Revelation 21:3–4 describes the absence of sorrow in heaven.
3. Describe the joy of God's presence as the central blessing of heaven.
4. Understand how eternal life guarantees lasting happiness.
5. Appreciate the fellowship of the redeemed as part of heaven's all-inclusive joy.

Introduction

HAVE YOU EVER PLANNED THE PERFECT VACATION? The hotel
was beautiful, the food was good, and the beach or mountains were
everything you hoped for. But then the weather turned bad, or you
got sick, or the trip ended too soon. Even in our best moments here,
happiness is fragile. Something always seems to break in.

We live in a world where joy comes and goes. A good day can be ruined
with one phone call. The excitement of success can be overshadowed by
worry about tomorrow. Even the sweetest memories are tinged with the
knowledge that they will not last. The Bible reminds us that "man is born
for trouble as surely as sparks fly upward" (Job 5:7). No one escapes it.

But the vision of heaven is different. There, happiness will not be fragile
or fleeting. It will be complete, secure, and permanent. Revelation 21:4
promises that God Himself will wipe away every tear. Death, grief,
crying, and pain, the very things that rob us of joy now, will be gone
forever.

This lesson calls us to see heaven as a place where happiness is not partial
or limited. It is all inclusive. Every longing of the heart will be met. Every
source of sorrow will be removed. And every child of God will share in a
joy that can never be taken away (John 16:22).

The Absence of Sorrow

*He will wipe away every tear from their eyes. Death will be no more; grief,
crying, and pain will be no more, because the previous things have passed
away,* Revelation 21:4.

From the Text
1. **No more sorrow.**
   One of the most significant barriers to lasting happiness on earth is

sorrow. Loss, disappointment, and pain are woven into human life. No matter how joyful the moment, something always lingers in the background to remind us it won't last. But John's vision of heaven assures us that all sorrow will be gone forever.

2. **All pain is gone.**

   This is more than the absence of pain; it is the tender promise that God Himself will remove the very causes of it. He will personally wipe away the tears. The Father will not delegate this comfort. His presence guarantees healing and relief.

Application

- Think about the weight of that promise. Death, which steals away those we love, will not enter the gates of heaven. Suffering, which now mars our bodies and minds, will be gone. Fear, which haunts us about tomorrow, will be silenced. Happiness in heaven is all-inclusive because sorrow will be excluded.
- Isaiah 25:8 foreshadows this when it declares, *He will swallow up death forever. The Lord God will wipe away the tears from every face.* And Psalm 30:5 reminds us, *Weeping may stay overnight, but there is joy in the morning.* Heaven is that eternal morning, where the night of sorrow never returns.

The Presence of God

Look, God's dwelling is with humanity, and He will live with them. They will be His peoples, and God Himself will be with them and will be their God, Revelation 21:3.

From the Text

1. **Face to Face … with the Father.**

   True happiness is not just about what is missing in heaven; it is about who is there. The greatest joy of the redeemed will be the presence of God Himself. On earth, even in our closest moments with the Lord, we still walk by faith and not by sight (2 Corinthians

5:7). We pray, we worship, and we trust, but we do not yet see Him face to face. In heaven, that will change. Revelation 22:4 promises, *They will see His face, and His name will be on their foreheads.* The barrier between the seen and unseen will be gone.

2. **Happiness is in God Himself.**
   Psalm 73:25–26 says: *Who do I have in heaven but You? And I desire nothing on earth but You. My flesh and my heart may fail, but God is the strength of my heart, my portion forever.* The psalmist recognized that happiness is not rooted in things, but in God Himself.

Application
- Our happiness in heaven will be perfected because it will come from direct communion with the Father and the Lamb.
- Every desire will be satisfied in His presence. Every need will be met. Every heart will be full.
- Earthly joy fades because people disappoint and possessions decay. Heavenly joy endures because it flows from the eternal God who never fails.

The Security of Eternal Life

"There is a time to be born and a time to die," Ecclesiastes 3:2.

From the Text
1. **Here, nothing lasts.**
   One reason happiness is fragile on earth is that nothing lasts. Health fades, relationships change, possessions wear out, and even our best moments slip away. Death stands as the great interrupter. And with death, earthly happiness comes to an end. There is … *a time to die.*

2. **Heaven changes everything.**
   Jesus said of His sheep, *I give them eternal life, and they will never perish. No one will snatch them out of my hand* (John 10:28). Happiness in heaven is secure because life there is eternal. Nothing can interrupt it.

3. **Nothing can diminish it.**

   Peter described our hope as *an inheritance that is imperishable, undefiled, and unfading, kept in heaven for you* (1 Peter 1:4). Notice the words: *imperishable, undefiled, unfading.* Everything on earth is perishable, defiled, and fading. But heaven's joy is untouched by time, sin, or decay. Paul speaks of this in Romans 6:23: *The wages of sin is death, but the gift of God is eternal life in Christ Jesus our Lord.*

Application

- Eternal life means eternal happiness. We will never fear losing it. The smile of heaven will never fade into sorrow.
- In heaven, happiness is all-inclusive because it is everlasting. The joy that begins there will never be threatened, interrupted, or lost.

The Fellowship of the Redeemed

A vast multitude from every nation, tribe, people, and language, which no one could number, standing before the throne and before the Lamb. They were clothed in white robes with palm branches in their hands. And they cried out in a loud voice: Salvation belongs to our God, who is seated on the throne, and to the Lamb!, Revelation 7:9–10.

From the Text

1. **Happiness is always greater when it is shared.**

   Some of our most joyful moments in life are not experienced alone but with people we love. Family gatherings, reunions with old friends, or celebrations with fellow Christians bring a taste of what heaven will be like. But here on earth, those moments end. Friends move away. Loved ones pass on. Even good relationships can be strained.

2. **In heaven, fellowship will be perfect and unbroken.**

   What a picture of unity and joy, God's children from every age and every corner of the earth, together at last.

Application

- Jesus promised in Matthew 8:11, *Many will come from east and west to share the banquet with Abraham, Isaac, and Jacob in the kingdom of heaven.* Imagine sitting at that table, reunited with loved ones who died in Christ, and joined by faithful saints you've only read about in Scripture. The joy of fellowship will be complete.
- Hebrews 12:22–23 adds that we have come to *the assembly of the firstborn whose names have been written in heaven.* That assembly will be filled with perfect love, free of jealousy, envy, or division. The fellowship of heaven will be unbreakable and eternal.
- Happiness in heaven is all-inclusive because it will be shared by every redeemed soul, perfected in Christ, forever united in love and praise.

Conclusion

The happiness we long for in this life always slips through our fingers. It is fragile, temporary, and often overshadowed by sorrow. But heaven is different. There, every tear will be wiped away. Pain, grief, and death will be no more. God Himself will be with us, and in His presence is fullness of joy. Eternal life will secure our happiness forever, free from the fear of loss. And we will share it, side by side with all the redeemed.

Heaven's happiness is not partial or exclusive. It is complete. It is unending. It is shared by all who belong to Christ. Jesus said, *You now have sorrow, but I will see you again. Your hearts will rejoice, and no one will take away your joy from you* (John 16:22). That is the promise of heaven.

So, we live in hope. Whatever trials we face, whatever disappointments come, we fix our eyes on the city where happiness is all-inclusive, where joy will never fade, and sorrow will never return.

For Discussion

1. Why is earthly happiness always temporary and fragile? What examples from your own life show this truth?

   _____

   _____

   _____

2. How does Revelation 21:4 comfort you personally when you think about loss, grief, or pain?

   _____

   _____

   _____

3. In what ways will the direct presence of God (Revelation 21:3; 22:4) be the most significant source of happiness in heaven?

   _____

   _____

   _____

4. How does the promise of eternal life (John 10:28; 1 Peter 1:4) change the way we view the ups and downs of life today?

   _____

   _____

   _____

5. What excites you most about the fellowship of heaven—the joy of reunion, the unity of those in Christ, or the presence of saints from every age and nation? Why?

   _____

   _____

   _____

Inconceivable Privileges

Revelation 22:3–5

And there will no longer be any curse. The throne of God and of the Lamb will be in the city, and his servants will worship him. They will see his face, and his name will be on their foreheads. Night will be no more; people will not need the light of a lamp or the light of the sun, because the Lord God will give them light, and they will reign forever and ever, Revelation 22:3–5.

Class Overview: In this lesson, we see heaven as the place of complete and lasting joy. Unlike the fragile happiness of this life, heaven offers an all-inclusive happiness where every sorrow is removed, God's presence is fully realized, eternal life secures our joy forever, and fellowship with the redeemed is perfect. The vision of Revelation 21–22 reminds us that in heaven, nothing will be missing. Every longing of the soul will be satisfied, and every child of God will share in joy that can never be taken away.

Class Objectives:
By the end of this class, you should be able to:
1. Explain why earthly happiness is temporary and incomplete.
2. Identify how Revelation 21:3–4 describes the absence of sorrow in heaven.
3. Describe the joy of God's presence as the central blessing of heaven.
4. Understand how eternal life guarantees lasting happiness.
5. Appreciate the fellowship of the redeemed as part of heaven's all-inclusive joy.

Introduction

I REMEMBER STANDING AT THE EDGE OF THE GRAND CANYON FOR THE FIRST TIME. Pictures I had seen all my life did not prepare me for the vastness, the depth, or the beauty that stretched before my eyes. I couldn't take it all in. Words failed. That moment taught me that some experiences are simply beyond description.

Heaven will be like that, only far greater. John, in Revelation 21–22, strains for words as he tries to describe the privileges of life in the eternal city. Gates of pearl. Streets of gold. Water of life. Yet behind those images lies a reality that cannot be fully captured. Paul reminds us, *What no eye has seen, no ear has heard, and no human heart has conceived—God has prepared these things for those who love him* (1 Corinthians 2:9).

Think about the privileges hinted at: seeing God's face, bearing His name, sharing His glory, and serving Him without sin or weakness. These are blessings we only glimpse now in part, but in the city of God they will be ours in full. Every promise of God will reach its completion. Every longing of the soul will be satisfied.

In this lesson, we will reflect on those inconceivable privileges: the inheritance of the saints, the honor of being called God's children, and the joy of eternal fellowship with Him. These are not distant dreams, but certain realities promised to all who belong to Christ.

We Will See His Face

And there will no longer be any curse. The throne of God and of the Lamb will be in the city, and his servants will worship him. They will see his face, and his name will be on their foreheads (Revelation 22:3–4).

From the Text
1. **In this world, no one can see God fully and live (Exodus 33:20).**
   His glory is too great for mortal eyes. Even Moses could only see

the afterglow of His presence. But in heaven, that barrier will be removed. John says: *They will see his face, and his name will be on their foreheads.* To see the face of God is to know Him without distance, without fear, without limitation.

2. **Perfect fellowship, the way we were created to live in the beginning.**

   This is not a privilege for angels alone; it belongs to the redeemed. God will welcome His children into His presence, where there is no more curse, no more sin, and no more separation. 1 John 3:2 ties this together: *We will be like him because we will see him as he is.* The vision of God transforms us into His likeness.

Application

- Think of the joy of seeing a loved one after a long absence. Multiply that by eternity, and you begin to touch the privilege of seeing God's face.
- All the questions, the struggles, the dark nights of faith will give way to the light of His presence.

We Will Share His Glory

The Spirit himself testifies together with our spirit that we are God's children, and if children, also heirs—heirs of God and coheirs with Christ—if indeed we suffer with him so that we may also be glorified with him, for I consider that the sufferings of this present time are not worth comparing with the glory that is going to be revealed to us, (Romans 8:16–18).

From the Text

1. **His inheritance becomes ours.**

   Paul says we are "children of God, and if children, also heirs: heirs of God and coheirs with Christ" (Romans 8:16–17).

2. **The glory Christ now has, we will share.**

   When Christ, who is your life, appears, then you also will appear with him in glory (Colossians 3:4). The sufferings of this life cannot compare with the glory that is coming (Romans 8:18). Every tear, trial, and loss will fade in the presence of eternal honor. This glory is not something we achieve. It is given to us by God's grace. We are lifted into a place of privilege not because of who we are, but because of who we belong to.

3. **In heaven, shame will be gone forever.**
    The redeemed will be clothed in honor, shining like the sun in the Father's kingdom (Matthew 13:43).

Application

- In this world, many of God's people live in obscurity, misunderstood or even despised. But in the city of God, every child of His will be honored.
- Imagine hearing the Father say, "Well done." Imagine sharing in the glory of the Son forever.

We Will Serve Him Without Weakness or Sin

How much more will the blood of Christ, who through the eternal Spirit offered himself without blemish to God, cleanse our consciences from dead works so that we can serve the living God, Hebrews 9:14.

From the Text

1. **Unimpeded, uninterrupted worship.**
    John tells us: *His servants will worship him* (Revelation 22:3). Service will not end in heaven; it will be perfected. Right now, our service is hindered by weakness, distraction, and sin. We grow tired. We get discouraged. Even at our best, we fall short. In the city of God, those barriers will be gone. No curse. No sin nature pulling us away. Our worship will be pure. Our service will be joyful. This will not be servitude that diminishes us, but service that fulfills us. In heaven, to serve is the highest privilege.

2. **A complete cleansing.**

Hebrews 9:14 says the blood of Christ cleanses our conscience "from dead works so that we can serve the living God." That cleansing will be complete in heaven.

Application

- Think of the frustration you've felt when you wanted to do more for the Lord but were limited by time, health, or energy.
- In heaven, none of those limits remain. We will give ourselves fully to God without weariness, and that will be our delight.

We Will Reign with Christ Forever

Night will be no more; people will not need the light of a lamp or the light of the sun, because the Lord God will give them light, and they will reign forever and ever, (Revelation 22:5).

From the Text

1. **Co-rulers with the King.**

John closes his vision by saying, *They will reign forever and ever* (Revelation 22:5). The redeemed are not only citizens of the city, but co-rulers with the King. This fulfills what Paul wrote: *If we endure, we will also reign with him* (2 Timothy 2:12). Our perseverance now leads to shared authority then. In Genesis, humanity was created to rule over God's creation (Genesis 1:26). Sin frustrated that purpose. In heaven, it will be restored.

2. **We share in His victory.**

This reign does not put us on God's level but allows us to share in His victory. We reign because Christ reigns, and we belong to Him.

3. **This reign is eternal.**

Unlike the rise and fall of earthly kingdoms, the kingdom of God will never end (Daniel 7:27).

Application

- Here we often feel powerless, at the mercy of sickness, governments, or circumstances. But in heaven, we will share in Christ's triumph.
- Imagine the honor of reigning with the One who conquered death. That is an inconceivable privilege.

Conclusion

When John closes Revelation, he is not trying to satisfy curiosity; he is trying to give hope. He shows us a city where God's people enjoy privileges too wonderful for human imagination: seeing His face, sharing His glory, serving without weakness, and reigning with Christ forever. These are not empty dreams. They are promises secured by the blood of the Lamb.

Think of what this means for your life right now. Whatever you suffer, however unnoticed your service may be, however weak you sometimes feel, none of it will last. God has prepared privileges beyond description for His children. Paul said: *The sufferings of this present time are not worth comparing with the glory that is going to be revealed to us* (Romans 8:18).

Heaven is not just a doctrine to discuss. It is our destiny. It is our inheritance. It is our joy. And when we get there, words will fail, for we will stand in the presence of God, overwhelmed by privileges beyond all thought, forever.

For Discussion

1. John says, "They will see his face" (Revelation 22:4). What does that privilege mean to you personally, and how does it compare with our relationship with God right now?

   _____

   _____

   _____

2. Romans 8:16–18 speaks of believers as "heirs of God and coheirs with Christ." How does the promise of sharing in Christ's glory encourage you when facing present trials?

   _____

   _____

   _____

3. Revelation 22:3 says His servants will worship Him. How is service in heaven different from the service we offer now, and why will it be a source of joy rather than weariness?

   _____

   _____

   _____

4. What does it mean that we will "reign forever and ever" with Christ (Revelation 22:5)? How should this future reality shape the way we view earthly power and kingdoms?

   _____

   _____

   _____

5. Of the privileges we've studied, seeing God's face, sharing His glory, serving Him without weakness, and reigning with Christ, which one stirs your heart the most, and why?

   _____

   _____

   _____

Eternal Light
Revelation 21:22–25; 22:5

I did not see a temple in it, because the Lord God the Almighty and the Lamb are its temple. The city does not need the sun or the moon to shine on it, because the glory of God illuminates it, and its lamp is the Lamb. The nations will walk by its light, and the kings of the earth will bring their glory into it. Its gates will never close by day, because it will never be night there, Revelation 21:22–25

Night will be no more; people will not need the light of a lamp or the light of the sun, because the Lord God will give them light, and they will reign forever and ever, Revelation 22:5.

Class Overview: Heaven is pictured as a city that needs no sun or moon, because the glory of God and the Lamb supply unending light (Revelation 21:23; 22:5). This lesson explores the meaning of that eternal light—God as the source, Christ as the lamp, the end of night, and our present call to live as children of light. In heaven, darkness with all its fears and sins will be banished forever, replaced with the unbroken joy and clarity of God's presence. Until that day, we reflect His light now, walking in holiness and hope as we await the eternal dawn.

Class Objectives:
By the end of this class, you should be able to:
1. Understand that God Himself is the source of light in heaven (Rev. 21:23).
2. Recognize the role of Christ, the Lamb, as the lamp of that eternal city.
3. Explain the significance of "no more night" in Revelation 22:5.

4. Apply the call to live as children of light in the present world (Ephesians 5:8).
5. Find hope in the promise of eternal safety, joy, and clarity in the presence of God.

Introduction

WHEN I WAS A BOY, MY FAMILY OWNED LAND OUTSIDE OF TOWN near the Ouachita River in southwest Arkansas. It was a great place to fish, swim, and gather with friends and family. On summer nights by the riverbank, cicadas hummed, and the stars felt close enough to touch. It was just a short walk from the rock bar down a trail through the woods to the truck. But on cloudy nights, the darkness in those thick woods was overwhelming. The dark felt heavy, and I worried about what might be hiding out of sight. When I remembered my parents weren't far away, my fear eased, and I felt safe. My dad would always make sure I was protected from any danger.

We all know what it feels like to long for light in the darkness. Darkness can be scary because it hides dangers and creates uncertainty. That's why Scripture often uses darkness as a symbol of sin, sorrow, and separation from God. Conversely, light stands for God's presence, truth, and salvation.

In the vision John saw of heaven, he describes a city that doesn't need the sun or the moon. Why? Because *the glory of God illuminates it, and its lamp is the Lamb* (Revelation 21:23). In heaven, there will never be night again. Shadows of fear, temptation, and death will disappear forever.

This lesson will help us think about what it means to live in that eternal light. It is more than physical brightness…it is the reality of God's presence, Christ's glory, and a life without darkness of any kind.

God is the Source of Eternal Light

The city does not need the sun or the moon to shine on it, because the glory of God illuminates it, and its lamp is the Lamb (Revelation 21:23).

From The Text

1. **Forever in the brightness of His presence.**
   When John describes the heavenly city, the very first detail he mentions about its light is powerful. There will be no sun, no moon, no lamp. Instead, the glory of God Himself will shine and fill every corner. From the first page of Scripture to the last, God reveals Himself as light: pure, holy, and life-giving. In heaven, that reality will be complete. We will live forever where no shadow can remain.

2. **God has always revealed Himself as light.**
   Psalm 27:1: *The Lord is my light and my salvation—whom should I fear?* 1 John 1:5: *God is light, and there is absolutely no darkness in him.* Psalm 36:9: *For with you is the fountain of life; in your light we will see light.*

3. **Implications of God's light.**
   Darkness cannot exist in His presence. On earth, we depend on the sun; in heaven, we rely entirely on God. His light means truth, holiness, and security. No confusion, no moral gray areas… everything will be seen clearly.

Application

- Even now, we walk in the light of God through Christ (John 8:12).
- The eternal city will bring this to its fullness… no more shadow, fear, or uncertainty.

The Lamb is the Lamp

The glory of God illuminates it, and its lamp is the Lamb, Revelation 21:23.

From The Text

1. **The light of heaven is personal.**
    The Lamb, Jesus Christ, is the lamp through which the glory of God shines. Just as a lamp spreads light into every corner of a room, Christ fills the eternal city with the radiance of God's presence.

2. **Christ is the Light of the world.**
    John 8:12: *I am the light of the world. Anyone who follows me will never walk in the darkness but will have the light of life.* John 1:4–5: *In him was life, and that life was the light of men. That light shines in the darkness, and yet the darkness did not overcome it.* The light of Christ will never fade, never be blocked, never be overcome.

3. **The Lamb's Role in Heaven.**
    He is central to heaven's glory because He purchased it with His blood (Revelation 5:9). His sacrifice makes it possible for us to dwell in God's light. Heaven is not heaven without the Lamb… it is His presence that makes it home.

Application

-   The light of heaven is not impersonal brightness … it is Christ Himself.
-   Eternity is not simply about "where" we are, but "with whom" we are.
-   The One who is our light now will be our lamp forever.

No More Night

Night will be no more; people will not need the light of a lamp or the light of the sun, because the Lord God will give them light, and they will reign forever and ever, (Revelation 22:5).

From the Text

1. **Night will never fall again.**
   Night in Scripture often represents danger, sorrow, or sin. The cycle of day and night that marks our lives here on earth will be over, replaced by the unbroken light of God's presence.

2. **Biblical themes of night.**
   John 3:19: *People loved darkness rather than the light because their deeds were evil.* Romans 13:12: *The night is nearly over, and the day is near.* Night is linked with sin, fear, confusion, and the absence of God's presence.

3. **The end of night in Heaven.**
   No fear of what lurks in the dark. No sorrow, grief, or uncertainty. No sin or temptation. Darkness has no place there. God's glory makes night unnecessary, and His presence makes it impossible.

Application

- Heaven is a place of perfect safety; nothing hidden, nothing threatening.
- Heaven is a place of unending joy; no shadows, no more endings, only light.
- Heaven is a place of rest and freedom. There will be no more watching, no more waiting, only dwelling secure in God's light.

Living in the Light

Night will be no more; people will not need the light of a lamp or the light of the sun, because the Lord God will give them light, and they will reign forever and ever, (Revelation 22:5).

From the Text
1. **A present calling.**
    Because God is light, and Christ is the lamp, we are already called to live as children of light in this dark world. Our present walk is meant to reflect the eternal reality we will one day enjoy in full.

2. **Called to walk in the light.**
    John 8:12: *I am the light of the world. Anyone who follows me will never walk in the darkness but will have the light of life.* Ephesians 5:8: *For you were once darkness, but now you are light in the Lord. Walk as children of light.* 1 Thessalonians 5:4–5: *You are all children of light and children of the day. We do not belong to the night or the darkness.*

3. **Practical implications for now:**
    We reflect the light of Christ by holy living. We resist the darkness of sin by holding to the truth. We shine God's light into the world by love and good works (Matthew 5:14–16).

Application
- One day we will no longer walk *toward* the light… we will live *in* the light.
- The struggle against darkness will be over.
- Our lives will be fully united with the glory of God forever.

Conclusion

The picture John paints of heaven is breathtaking. No sun, no moon, no night…only the radiant glory of God shining through the Lamb. Darkness, with all its fears and dangers, will be gone forever. What a hope!

We often struggle with the shadows here: confusion, sorrow, sin, and uncertainty. But Revelation reminds us that God Himself is our light. Jesus, the Lamb, is the lamp. And in His presence, nothing unclean or threatening can exist. Eternal light means eternal safety, eternal joy, and eternal clarity.

But this vision also calls us to live differently now. We are already children of light, walking in a dark world (Ephesians 5:8). Our lives must reflect the eternal reality that awaits us. The way we live, the way we speak, the way we love others… it all becomes a testimony of the light of Christ shining through us.

Heaven will be a place of unbroken light, and for those in Christ, that light has already dawned in our hearts. So, we live today with anticipation, and we long for the day when night will be no more, and the Lord Himself will give us light.

For Discussion

1. When you think about darkness, what feelings or experiences come to mind? How does that help us understand why Scripture uses darkness as a picture of sin and fear?

   _____

   _____

   _____

2. Revelation 21:23 says the city does not need the sun or the moon. What does this teach us about the sufficiency of God's glory?

   _____

   _____

   _____

3. Why do you think John describes Jesus as "the lamp" of the city? How does this connect with what He said in John 8:12?

   _____

   _____

   _____

4. Revelation 22:5 says, "Night will be no more." What does that mean practically for our understanding of heaven?

_____

_____

_____

5. How does the promise of eternal light give you comfort when facing the "dark nights" of life right now?

_____

_____

_____

6. Ephesians 5:8 says, "Walk as children of light." What are some practical ways we can reflect Christ's light in our daily lives?

_____

_____

_____

7. How can remembering the eternal light of heaven change the way we deal with temptation, sorrow, or uncertainty in the present?

_____

_____

_____

God's Eternal Presence

Revelation 21:23

The city does not need the sun or the moon to shine on it, because the glory of God illuminates it, and its lamp is the Lamb (Revelation 21:23).

Class Overview: Heaven's greatest blessing is not its beauty or rewards but the eternal presence of God. From Eden to the tabernacle, from the temple to Christ Himself, Scripture reveals God's desire to dwell with His people. In the eternal city, that longing will be fully realized—no more separation, no more night, no more curse. God Himself will be our light, our security, and our joy. This lesson reminds us that what makes heaven truly heaven is not the place, but the presence of God.

Class Objectives:
By the end of this class, you should be able to:
1. Trace the theme of God's presence throughout Scripture and see its fulfillment in heaven.
2. Explain why God's presence—not material images of heaven—is the greatest blessing of eternity.
3. Identify what "night" symbolizes in Scripture and how its end points to God's eternal light and security.
4. Apply the hope of God's eternal presence to daily life, finding courage, strength, and joy in His nearness now.
5. Deepen their longing for heaven by recognizing that the ultimate promise is to see God's face and dwell with Him forever.

Introduction

WHEN I WAS A CHILD, I SPENT A LOT OF TIME AT MY GRANDPARENTS' HOUSE. It was a typical 1970s ranch-style home in a subdivision. It sat on a cul-de-sac at the top of a hill. They owned multiple lots with woods on either side, and behind them sat an old homestead. The backyard had been cleared of the woods, but many trees remained standing. They had an above-ground swimming pool and plenty of space for me to play. Even though we were in town, it felt like we were in the country.

But what made it truly special was them…their presence. I can still hear their voices, smell my grandmother's cooking, and remember all the fun I had there. This year marks thirty years since they left that house to move in with my parents, where they lived for a few years. My grandfather passed away in 1997, and my grandmother in 2016. I still think of them often. Whenever I return to Arkansas, I usually drive past their old place. It seems much smaller than I remember, and the truth is, it simply isn't the same. As I reflect, I realize it was never about the place; it was about who was there.

That's how heaven is. It isn't the streets of gold or the gates of pearl that make it glorious. The beauty of the city is not its true treasure. The absolute joy of heaven is that **God Himself will be there.** Revelation 21:3 declares, *Look, God's dwelling is with humanity, and he will live with them. They will be his peoples, and God himself will be with them and will be their God.* That is the promise. Heaven will be heaven because we will live in the eternal presence of God.

God Has Always Desired to Dwell with His People

The city does not need the sun or the moon to shine on it, because the glory of God illuminates it, and its lamp is the Lamb (Revelation 21:23).

From the Text
1. **God's greatest gift to His people is His presence.**
   In Eden, God walked with Adam and Eve in the cool of the day (Genesis 3:8). When sin broke that fellowship, humanity was

driven away (Genesis 3:23–24). Yet the story of the Bible is God working to draw near again. He dwelt among Israel in the tabernacle and temple (Exodus 25:8; 1 Kings 8:10–11). In Christ, "the Word became flesh and dwelt among us" (John 1:14). And today, His Spirit lives in His people (1 Corinthians 3:16). All these point forward to heaven, where His presence will never be broken again (Revelation 21:3).

2. **Biblical themes of God's presence:**
   God's presence meant blessing and peace for Israel (Numbers 6:24–26). His presence gave strength and courage in times of fear (Joshua 1:9). Sin separated man from God, but His plan has always been restoration (Isaiah 59:2; Jeremiah 31:33). Jesus came as Immanuel, "God with us" (Matthew 1:23), the clearest expression of God's desire to dwell among His people.

3. The fulfillment in Heaven.
   No more barriers of sin or separation. No more symbols (tabernacle, temple) to remind us ... God Himself will be there. Revelation 21:3–4: God will dwell with His people, wipe away every tear, and remove death and pain forever.

Application

- Heaven is not just about beauty or reward: it is about God Himself.
- Our deepest longing will be fulfilled in His presence.
- As Christians, we should now hunger for fellowship with God, knowing that heaven will be the complete realization of what we taste here on earth.

God's Presence is the Greatest Blessing of Heaven

Look, God's dwelling is with humanity, and he will live with them. They will be his peoples, and God himself will be with them and will be their God, (Revelation 21:3).

From the Text

1. **His presence will be the source of every blessing and the center of all joy.**

2. **Biblical themes of God's presence as blessing:**
   Psalm 16:11: *In your presence is abundant joy; at your right hand are eternal pleasures.* Psalm 73:25–26: Nothing on earth compares to being near God. Exodus 33:14–15: Moses refused to go without God's presence, showing that His presence is more valuable than any earthly land or promise. Revelation 22:4: *They will see his face.* The ultimate blessing is to behold God without fear.

3. **The experience of His presence in Heaven:**
   Every joy of heaven flows from God Himself. His presence will bring unbroken fellowship and endless delight. No temple will be needed, for "the Lord God the Almighty and the Lamb are its temple" (Revelation 21:22). His presence will be personal… we will see Him face to face (1 John 3:2).

Application

- Heaven is heaven because God is there. Without Him, even paradise would be empty.
- The Christian life now should reflect this hunger for His presence through worship, prayer, and holiness.
- Anticipating heaven means cultivating joy in God now, knowing the greatest blessing is not the place, but the Person.

God's Presence Brings Eternal Security and Rest

And there will no longer be any curse. The throne of God and of the Lamb will be in the city, and his servants will worship him, (Revelation 22:3).

From the Text

1. **Security from His presence.**
    Revelation 22:3–5 promises a life where the curse is gone, His servants serve Him, they see His face, and they reign with Him forever. No more threats, no more enemies, no more curse… only the safety and rest of His eternal presence.

2. **Biblical themes of security in God's presence:**
    Psalm 23:4: *I will fear no danger, for you are with me.* Psalm 46:1: God is our refuge and strength, a helper always found in times of trouble. Isaiah 32:18: God's people will dwell in peaceful places, in secure dwellings, in quiet resting places. John 10:28: No one can snatch God's people from His hand.

3. **The experience of His presence in Heaven:**
    The curse of sin and death is removed forever (Revelation 22:3). No more separation, sorrow, or danger: perfect rest in God's presence. Eternal reign with God means no enemy can rise against His people again. His face will be the constant assurance of His love and protection.

Application

*   Heaven is the end of fear—no more uncertainty, no more waiting for relief… only safety in God's presence.
*   Heaven is the end of the struggle. The fight against sin, temptation, and weakness will be over.
*   Heaven is the beginning of perfect rest. To be with God forever means unbroken peace and eternal security.

Conclusion

The greatest joy of heaven is not found in the beauty of the city or the blessings it holds. The true glory of heaven is that *God will be there.* From the first pages of Scripture, God has shown His desire to dwell with His people. Sin separated us, but His plan of redemption has consistently pointed to the day when separation would end.

In heaven, there will be no more night, no more fear, no more curse. God's presence will fill every corner. His face will be our light. His nearness will be our security. His fellowship will be our joy.

When we think about heaven, it is easy to get caught up in the pictures of gold, gates, and beauty. But if those things were there and God was not, it would not be heaven. What makes heaven heaven is the eternal presence of our God. And that is the promise that gives us hope now and forever.

For Discussion

1. When you think about heaven, what images or ideas come to mind first? How does Revelation 21:3 help reframe our focus?

    _____

    _____

    _____

2. In what ways did God make His presence known to His people in the Old Testament (tabernacle, temple, etc.)? How do those points forward to heaven?

    _____

    _____

    _____

3. How does Jesus, as Immanuel ("God with us"), show us God's desire to dwell among His people?

_____

_____

_____

4. Revelation 22:5 says, *"Night will be no more."* What does "night" represent in Scripture, and why is its removal so necessary?

_____

_____

_____

5. How does the promise of God's eternal presence give us strength to endure trials and temptations now?

_____

_____

_____

6. If heaven's greatest blessing is being with God, how should that shape our priorities and values today?

_____

_____

_____

7. Why do you think Scripture emphasizes seeing God's face (Revelation 22:4; 1 John 3:2)? What does that reveal about the kind of relationship we will have with Him?

_____

_____

_____

Eternal Fellowship

Revelation 7:9–10

After this, I looked, and there was a vast multitude from every nation, tribe, people, and language, which no one could number, standing before the throne and before the Lamb. They were clothed in white robes with palm branches in their hands. And they cried out in a loud voice: Salvation belongs to our God, who is seated on the throne, and to the Lamb, (Revelation 7:9–10).

Class Overview: Heaven's greatest blessing is not its beauty or rewards but the eternal presence of God. From Eden to the tabernacle, from the temple to Christ Himself, Scripture reveals God's desire to dwell with His people. In the eternal city, that longing will be fully realized— no more separation, no more night, no more curse. God Himself will be our light, our security, and our joy. This lesson reminds us that what makes heaven truly heaven is not the place, but the presence of God.

Class Objectives:
By the end of this class, you should be able to:
1. Trace the theme of God's presence throughout Scripture and see its fulfillment in heaven.
2. Explain why God's presence—not material images of heaven—is the greatest blessing of eternity.
3. Identify what "night" symbolizes in Scripture and how its end points to God's eternal light and security.
4. Apply the hope of God's eternal presence to daily life, finding courage, strength, and joy in His nearness now.
5. Deepen their longing for heaven by recognizing that the ultimate promise is to see God's face and dwell with Him forever.

Introduction

WHEN I WAS A BOY, EVERY FEW YEARS OUR EXTENDED FAMILY would gather in Greenwood, Arkansas, for a reunion. It was special. It was important to my grandmother. Twenty years before, her husband passed away in a matter of months after a diagnosis of cancer. This was his family, and she wanted to make sure my uncle, mom, and I would maintain a connection with them. Cousins, aunts, uncles, and grandparents would come in from all over Arkansas, Oklahoma, and Kansas. The day was filled with laughter, food, and stories that bound us together. But even as good as those times were, they always ended. People had to pack up, say their goodbyes, and head back to their separate lives.

Our experiences of fellowship in this life are always incomplete. Distance, time, sin, and even death eventually interrupt them. But God has promised something better. In heaven, all His people will finally be together … forever. No separation. No conflict. No goodbyes.

The Bible paints a picture of a great multitude gathered before the throne (Revelation 7:9–10). From every nation and generation, they are united in one voice of praise. This is the fellowship of God's sons and daughters in its fullest expression.

When we think about heaven, we rightly focus on being with God. But we should not overlook the joy of being reunited with one another —family, friends, saints across time —sharing in the unbroken communion of Christ's eternal city. That's the fellowship we are longing for.

The Gathering of the Redeemed

After this, I looked, and there was a vast multitude from every nation, tribe, people, and language, which no one could number, standing before the throne and before the Lamb, (Revelation 7:9).

From the Text

1. **All separations and barriers removed.**
    John's vision shows heaven filled with the redeemed of all ages, united before the throne and the Lamb. The barriers that divide us on earth — time, language, culture, death —are gone. What remains is one great assembly of God's people, perfected and gathered forever in His presence.

2. **Biblical themes of God's gathering:**
    Hebrews 12:22–23: The assembly of the firstborn, written in heaven, surrounding the throne of God. Matthew 8:11: Many will come from east and west to sit with Abraham, Isaac, and Jacob in the kingdom of heaven. 1 Thessalonians 4:17–18: *We will be caught up together with them … and so we will always be with the Lord*—John 10:16: One flock, one Shepherd.

3. **The experience of fellowship in Heaven:**
    Every believer across time and place will be present: patriarchs, prophets, apostles, and saints. Loved ones in Christ, long separated by death, will be reunited. A multitude from every nation will praise with one voice, clothed in white robes of victory. The redeemed will not just be individuals in God's presence, but one family, one city, one body.

Application

- Heaven is the end of separation—no more death, distance, or division … only eternal reunion.
- Heaven is the end of loneliness. We will belong, fully and forever, to God's family.
- Heaven is the fullness of fellowship. Our worship, joy, and service will be shared with all God's people.

Perfect Fellowship

They will see his face, and his name will be on their foreheads. Night will be no more; people will not need the light of a lamp or the light of the sun, because the Lord God will give them light, and they will reign forever and ever., (Revelation 22:4–5).

From the Text
1. **Perfect fellowship.**
   Fellowship on earth is fragile…sin, pride, misunderstandings, and weakness often strain relationships. In heaven, fellowship will be perfected. We will see God's face and bear His name—fully known and fully belonging. That perfect relationship with Him will overflow into perfect relationships with one another.
2. **Biblical themes of perfect fellowship:**
   Psalm 133:1: *How good and pleasant it is when brothers live together in harmony.* John 17:21: Jesus prayed that His followers *may all be one, as you, Father, are in me and I am in you.* Acts 2:42: The early church devoted themselves to the apostles' teaching, fellowship, the breaking of bread, and prayers: an earthly glimpse of heavenly unity. Ephesians 2:19: In Christ we are no longer strangers, but fellow citizens with the saints and members of God's household.
3. **The experience of fellowship in Heaven:**
   No sin will ever again divide God's people: no jealousy, no envy, no anger, no pride. Love will bind us perfectly, reflecting God's own love. Harmony will not be fragile or temporary, but permanent and complete. Every son or daughter of God will enjoy unbroken communion with the Father and one another.

Application
- Heaven is the end of conflict: no more strained friendships, broken homes, or church divisions.
- Heaven is the end of misunderstanding. Our relationships will be pure, transparent, and true.

- Heaven is the fullness of unity. What Jesus prayed for in John 17 will finally be realized forever.

Shared Joy

They sang a new song: You are worthy to take the scroll and to open its seals, because you were slaughtered, and you purchased people for God by your blood from every tribe and language and people and nation. You made them a kingdom and priests to our God, and they will reign on the earth., (Revelation 5:9–10).

From the Text
The picture of heaven is filled with joy expressed in worship. The redeemed lift their voices in a song that never ends, celebrating the Lamb who purchased them by His blood. Joy is not solitary—it is shared. Heaven is a place where God's people rejoice together in their salvation and in the eternal victory of Christ.

Biblical Themes of Shared Joy
- Psalm 16:11: "In your presence is abundant joy; at your right hand are eternal pleasures."
- Isaiah 35:10: God's ransomed will return with singing; everlasting joy will crown their heads.
- Luke 15:7: There is joy in heaven over one sinner who repents—a joy multiplied among the redeemed.
- Philippians 4:4: "Rejoice in the Lord always. I will say it again: Rejoice!"

The Experience of Joy in Heaven
- Worship will be a shared celebration: every voice raised in thanksgiving to God and the Lamb.
- Our joy will be multiplied because it is shared with countless others.
- No sorrow, grief, or disappointment will diminish our rejoicing.
- The victory of Christ will be the theme of every heart and song, forever.

Application

- Heaven is the end of sorrow. Tears will be replaced by gladness and singing.
- Heaven is the end of loneliness in joy. We will not rejoice alone but with all the redeemed.
- Heaven is the fullness of celebration. Together, we will forever praise the Lamb who made our joy complete.

Conclusion

Heaven is not only about seeing God face to face; it is about being gathered with His people in perfect fellowship and shared joy. What sin broke apart on earth, God will make whole forever. Every barrier, distance, culture, time, and even death will be removed. We will stand together as one family, united by the blood of Christ, rejoicing without end.

Think of what that means: no more goodbyes, no more misunderstandings, no more strained relationships. Only love. Only harmony. Only joy. The fellowship we taste here in the church is but a shadow of the eternal communion that awaits in the heavenly city.

The promise of heaven reminds us to value fellowship now. If we cannot live at peace with one another here, how can we hope to enjoy perfect fellowship there? Let us pursue unity, forgiveness, and love today, knowing that one day we will stand side by side in glory, forever in the presence of our God and with all the redeemed.

For Discussion

1. Revelation 7:9–10 shows a vast multitude before the throne. How does this vision shape the way you think about the church today?

   _____

   _____

   _____

2. What barriers divide people on earth that will be removed forever in heaven?

   _____

   _____

   _____

3. What kinds of sin most often damage our fellowship here on earth?

4. How does the promise of perfect unity in heaven challenge us to pursue unity in the church now?

   _____

   _____

   _____

5. Why do you think joy in heaven is pictured as something shared, not just individual?

   _____

   _____

   _____

6. How does worship here on earth serve as a foretaste of heaven's eternal joy?

   _____

   _____

   _____

7. How does the hope of eternal fellowship with all believers encourage you in times of loneliness or grief?

   _____

   _____

   _____

8. What steps can we take in our local congregation to reflect the heavenly fellowship we are promised?

_____

_____

_____

Eternal Worship

Revelation 7:11–12

All the angels stood around the throne, and along with the elders and the four living creatures, they fell face down before the throne and worshiped God, saying, Amen! Blessing and glory and wisdom and thanksgiving and honor and power and strength be to our God forever and ever. Amen,
Revelation 7:11–12.

Class Overview: Heaven is pictured as a place where worship never ends. Around the throne, the redeemed and all creation lift their voices in unceasing praise to God and the Lamb. This worship is focused entirely on Him—His holiness, His worth, and His saving power—and is filled with joy that cannot be diminished. In heaven, worship is not an event to attend but the atmosphere of eternal life. This lesson will help us see how our worship now is a foretaste of what is to come and challenge us to develop hearts that love to glorify God.

Class Objectives:
By the end of this class, you should be able to:
1. Describe the biblical vision of eternal worship in Revelation.
2. Explain why worship in heaven is unceasing, God-focused, and joyful.
3. Contrast earthly worship with the perfection of heavenly worship.
4. Apply the hope of eternal worship to present life, especially during times of sorrow and distraction.
5. Develop greater devotion to worshiping God now as preparation for eternity.

Introduction

Over the years, I have attended lectureships and conferences where thousands of people gathered in one place. As the singing began, the sound was almost overwhelming. Voices rose together, strong and clear, filling the building with praise to God. I remember thinking, *This must be just a small taste of heaven.* Worship here on earth can be profoundly moving, but it is always incomplete. Our voices grow tired. (*I can't sing like I could when I was younger.*) Our attention drifts. The demands of life eventually pull us away. Even the most powerful worship moments fade.

But Scripture gives us a picture of heaven where worship never ends. Revelation 7:9–12 describes a multitude that no one could number, from every nation, crying out together: *"Salvation belongs to our God, who is seated on the throne, and to the Lamb!"* In that city, worship will be unbroken, perfect, and eternal.

Heaven is not only a place of peace, fellowship, and rest: it is a place where God's people will give Him the glory He deserves forever. Worship will not be an event we attend, but the atmosphere of our eternal life with God.

Unceasing Praise

Day and night they never stop, saying: Holy, holy, holy, Lord God, the Almighty, who was, who is, and who is to come, (Revelation 4:8).

From the Text
John's vision of heaven shows worship that never ceases. The living creatures around the throne give glory without pause, declaring the holiness and majesty of God. Worship in heaven is not bound by time, weariness, or distraction. It is the constant response of created beings to the eternal worth of the Creator.

Biblical Themes of Unceasing Praise

- Psalm 113:3: "From the rising of the sun to its setting, let the name of the Lord be praised."
- Isaiah 6:3: The seraphim call to one another, "Holy, holy, holy is the Lord of Armies; his glory fills the whole earth."
- Hebrews 13:15: "Through him let us continually offer up to God a sacrifice of praise."
- Revelation 19:6: "Hallelujah, because our Lord God, the Almighty, reigns!"

The Experience of Worship in Heaven

- Worship will be continuous, not occasional: unceasing acknowledgment of God's greatness.
- Worship will be effortless and joyful: no fatigue, no wandering thoughts, no distractions.
- Worship will be universal: every voice and every creature united in adoration.
- Worship will be pure: no pride or hypocrisy, only truth and devotion.

Application

- Heaven reminds us that worship is not confined to one hour a week; it is the continual posture of a heart that sees God.
- Our worship on earth prepares us for eternal worship. Every song, prayer, and act of devotion points forward to that day.
- If we grow weary of praising God now, it challenges us to examine our hearts. Heaven is for those who love to worship.

The Focus of Heaven

They cast their crowns before the throne and say: Our Lord and God, you are worthy to receive glory and honor and power, because you have created all things, and by your will they exist and were created, (Revelation 4:10–11).

From the Text

The worship of heaven is centered entirely on God and the Lamb. The elders fall before Him, casting their crowns, acknowledging that all glory belongs to Him alone. Worship in heaven is not self-centered or man-focused—it is God-focused. The throne is the center of heaven's life and activity.

Biblical Themes of God-Centered Worship

- Exodus 15:11: "Lord, who is like you among the gods? Who is like you, glorious in holiness, revered with praises, performing wonders?"
- Psalm 29:2: "Ascribe to the Lord the glory due his name; worship the Lord in the splendor of his holiness."
- John 4:23–24: True worshipers will worship the Father in Spirit and in truth, for the Father seeks such as these.
- Philippians 2:10–11: Every knee will bow, and every tongue confess that Jesus Christ is Lord.

The Experience of Heaven's Focus

- All attention will be on the throne: no distractions, no competing affections.
- All glory will be directed to God: He alone is worthy.
- The Lamb who was slain will be exalted as Savior and King.
- Worship will be unified: not divided among denominations, cultures, or personal preferences.

Application

- Heaven reminds us that worship is not about us: it is about God.
- Worship is not measured by how it makes us feel but by whether God is honored.
- When we gather in worship now, we practice for eternity by learning to shift our focus from ourselves to Him.

The Joy of Worship

After this, I heard something like the loud voice of a vast multitude in heaven, saying: Hallelujah! Salvation, glory, and power belong to our God, because his judgments are true and righteous ... Then I heard something like the voice of a vast multitude, like the sound of cascading waters, and like the rumbling of loud thunder, saying: Hallelujah, because our Lord God, the Almighty, reigns, (Revelation 19:1–2, 6).

From the Text

The worship of heaven is marked by overwhelming joy. A vast multitude cries out "Hallelujah!" with the sound of rushing waters and rolling thunder. The joy of heaven is not silent or subdued: it is full, exuberant, and shared. Worship is the celebration of God's victory, salvation, and reign.

Biblical Themes of Joyful Worship
- Psalm 16:11: "In your presence is abundant joy; at your right hand are eternal pleasures."
- Psalm 100:2: "Serve the Lord with gladness; come before him with joyful songs."
- Isaiah 51:11: "The ransomed of the Lord will return and come to Zion with singing, crowned with unending joy."
- Luke 2:10 11: The angel announced, "I proclaim to you good news of great joy ... today a Savior was born for you."

The Experience of Joy in Heaven
- Every voice will be lifted in glad praise: joy unbroken and unending.
- Worship will not be hindered by sorrow, pain, or distraction.
- Joy will be multiplied because it is shared with the redeemed of all ages.
- The victory of God will be the theme of eternal rejoicing.

Application

- Heaven reminds us that true joy is found in God's presence, not in earthly circumstances.
- Worship now should reflect the gladness of eternity: praising with our hearts as well as our lips.
- If worship feels like a burden, heaven challenges us to rediscover the joy of honoring God.

Conclusion

Heaven is a place where worship never ends. Around the throne of God and the Lamb, every creature will lift its voice in unceasing praise, perfect focus, and overflowing joy. Worship will not be something we "go to," … it will be the very atmosphere of our eternal life.

Think of it: no distractions, no weariness, no divided hearts. Only glad voices, united together, honoring the One who saved us. The scenes of Revelation remind us that the center of heaven is not mansions, streets of gold, or gates of pearl: it is the throne of God. The joy of heaven is the joy of worshiping Him forever.

And this truth challenges us now. If we long for eternal worship, then our hearts must learn to treasure worship in the present. Every song sung, every prayer lifted, every word of Scripture read is a rehearsal for eternity. Worship here is preparation for the endless worship of heaven.

For Discussion

1. Revelation 4:8 describes worship that never stops. What does this teach us about the nature of worship in heaven?

    _____

    _____

    _____

2. Why do you think worship in heaven is continuous and not occasional?

    _____

    _____

    _____

3. Revelation 4:10–11 shows elders casting their crowns before God's throne. What does this action teach us about humility and focus in worship?

    _____

    _____

    _____

4. How is worship in heaven different from worship on earth in terms of focus and distractions?

    _____

    _____

    _____

5. Revelation 19:1–6 describes a multitude shouting "Hallelujah!" What does this reveal about the joy of heavenly worship?

    _____

    _____

    _____

6. How does the picture of unbroken, joyful worship in heaven encourage you during times of sorrow or hardship now?

    _____

    _____

    _____

7. What are some practical ways our worship on earth can better reflect the focus and joy of heaven?

_____

_____

_____

8. If heaven is filled with eternal worship, what does that reveal about the kind of hearts we need to be developing today?

_____

_____

_____

PART FOUR

The Fulfillment of Heaven

The final section of our study turns to the completion of God's promises: the peace, rest, and eternal security of heaven. Here we see the end of the journey—the moment when every longing of the faithful is satisfied in the presence of God. Heaven is not only a place of beauty and blessing; it is the final rest for the people of God, where sorrow, fear, and uncertainty are gone forever. In this fulfillment, the story of redemption reaches its climax as God's people live in unbroken communion with Him for all eternity.

Perfect Peace and Rest

Hebrews 4:9–11

Therefore, a Sabbath rest remains for God's people. For the person who has entered his rest has rested from his own works, just as God did from his. Let us, then, make every effort to enter that rest, so that no one will fall into the same pattern of disobedience, (Hebrews 4:9–11).

Class Overview: Heaven is the place where all struggle ends, and perfect peace begins. Scripture promises that God will wipe away every tear, remove death and sorrow, and welcome His people into eternal rest. The curse of sin and the weariness of life will be gone, replaced by the security of God's presence and the joy of His Sabbath rest. This lesson helps us see how heaven answers our deepest longings for relief, renewal, and safety, and encourages us to persevere with hope until that day.

Class Objectives:
By the end of this class, you should be able to:
1. Explain what Revelation 21:4 and related passages teach about the end of earthly struggle.
2. Describe the biblical vision of perfect peace in God's presence.
3. Define the "Sabbath rest" of Hebrews 4:9–11 and how it is fulfilled in heaven.
4. Contrast the temporary nature of earthly rest with the eternal rest of heaven.
5. Apply the hope of heaven's peace and rest to daily struggles, griefs, and trials.

Introduction

WHEN WE PURCHASED OUR PROPERTY A FEW YEARS AGO, the back acre and a half was overgrown with honeysuckle trees and brush. There were stands of thorn bushes and broken limbs from years of neglect. As fall began, I began clearing things by hand. Throughout the winter, the work continued—removing a section at a time. Days were filled with cutting trees, cutting firewood, piling branches and debris onto a burn pile. By early spring, it was done. But the work was exhausting. I can remember walking back to the house so worn out that I could barely think straight. My body ached, and all I wanted was a shower, then to collapse into a chair and rest. After some sleep, I felt better, but the rest never lasted. The next day brought out sore muscles, scratched skin, *and* more work to do. That's the way it is with earthly rest—it always runs out.

Thankfully, Scripture promises a rest that does not end. Revelation 14:13 says, *"Blessed are the dead who die in the Lord ... they will rest from their labors, since their works follow them."* Revelation 21:4 assures us that every tear will be wiped away, and pain, grief, and death will be gone forever. The eternal city is not marked by striving and struggle, but by peace and rest.

The peace of heaven is not just the absence of conflict: it is the presence of God Himself. It is safety, security, and joy in His presence. It is what Jesus promised when He said, *"Come to me ... and I will give you rest"* (Matthew 11:28).

Heaven is the home of perfect peace and everlasting rest. The struggles that wear us down now will be finished. The griefs that break our hearts will be healed. In God's presence, His people will rest secure forever.

The End of Struggle

He will wipe away every tear from their eyes. Death will be no more; grief, crying, and pain will be no more, because the previous things have passed away, (Revelation 21:4).

From the Text

John's vision assures us that in heaven, the struggles that define life on earth will finally end. Death, sorrow, pain, and tears, all marks of a broken world, will be gone forever. The curse that began in Eden is fully lifted in the eternal city.

Biblical Themes of the End of Struggle

- Isaiah 25:8: God will swallow up death forever and wipe away the tears from every face.
- Romans 8:18: "The sufferings of this present time are not worth comparing with the glory that is going to be revealed to us."
- 1 Corinthians 15:54–55: Death is swallowed up in victory.
- 2 Corinthians 4:17: Our momentary light affliction is producing an absolutely incomparable eternal weight of glory.

The Experience of Heaven's Rest

- No more sin to fight against. Temptation and weakness are gone.
- No more sorrow to endure. Grief, pain, and loss are healed.
- No more death to fear. Its power is broken forever.
- No more tears to shed. Every wound is healed by God's own hand.

Application

- Heaven is the end of weariness: no more long days, no more exhaustion of body or spirit.
- Heaven is the end of grief: no more loss, no more empty places at the table.
- Heaven is the end of fear: no more waiting for the next hardship or trial.

The Presence of Peace

My people will dwell in a peaceful place, in safe and secure dwellings, and in undisturbed resting places., (Isaiah 32:18).

From the Text

The peace of heaven is not simply the absence of conflict: it is the presence of God Himself. His presence assures safety, security, and calm. Isaiah's vision of God's people resting in secure dwellings finds its ultimate fulfillment in the heavenly city, where nothing can threaten or disturb them again.

Biblical Themes of Peace in God's Presence
- Psalm 4:8: "I will both lie down and sleep in peace, for you alone, Lord, make me live in safety."
- Psalm 23:2: "He leads me beside quiet waters. He renews my life."
- Philippians 4:7: The peace of God, which surpasses all understanding, will guard your hearts and minds in Christ Jesus.
- John 14:27: Jesus promised, "My peace I give to you. I do not give to you as the world gives."

The Experience of Peace in Heaven
- No danger to fear. God's protection is absolute.
- No unrest or anxiety. Perfect calm in His presence.
- No division or conflict. Complete harmony among all God's people.
- No insecurity. Dwelling in the unshakable kingdom of God.

Application
- Heaven reminds us that true peace is not found in circumstances but in God's presence.
- We should not be surprised when peace is fragile in this world; only in heaven will it be complete.

- When we trust God's promises now, we taste the peace that will one day be ours fully.
- Living with heaven in view helps us approach trials and conflict with steady hearts.

The Fulfillment of Rest

Therefore, a Sabbath rest remains for God's people. For the person who has entered his rest has rested from his own works, just as God did from his. Let us, then, make every effort to enter that rest, so that no one will fall into the same pattern of disobedience., (Hebrews 4:9–11).

From the Text

The Hebrew writer points to the promise of eternal rest as the ultimate goal of God's people. Just as God rested after creation, His people will enter His rest, complete, unbroken, and eternal. In heaven, the weariness of labor, the burdens of sin, and the trials of life are replaced by the joy of God's Sabbath rest.

Biblical Themes of God's Rest
- Exodus 33:14: "My presence will go with you, and I will give you rest."
- Matthew 11:28–29: Jesus invites the weary to find rest in Him.
- Revelation 14:13: "Blessed are the dead who die in the Lord… they will rest from their labors."
- Isaiah 57:2: "The one who walks uprightly enters into peace; they will rest on their beds."

The Experience of Rest in Heaven
- Rest from labor, our work and toil in a cursed world will be finished.
- Rest from sin and temptation, the battle is over.
- Rest from sorrow, grief, and pain will be no more.
- Rest in God, perfect contentment and refreshment in His presence.

Application

- Heaven is the answer to our deepest longings for relief and renewal.
- The rest Jesus gives us now is a foretaste of the eternal rest to come.
- Our labor and perseverance in Christ are not in vain; they lead to eternal reward.
- Striving faithfully today ensures we will share in God's Sabbath rest tomorrow.

Conclusion

Heaven is the home of perfect peace and everlasting rest. The struggles of life will be finished, the griefs of the heart will be healed, and the labor of a broken world will be over. God Himself will wipe away every tear, and His people will dwell securely in His presence.

On earth, peace is fragile, and rest is temporary. But in heaven, peace will never be disturbed, and rest will never end. It is the fulfillment of what Jesus promised when He said, *"Come to me … and I will give you rest."*

This promise calls us to endure faithfully now. Our present struggles, griefs, and labors are not the end of the story. God has prepared a place where His people will live in unshakable peace and eternal rest. That hope strengthens us today and points us forward to the everlasting joy of His presence.

For Discussion

1. Revelation 21:4 says God will wipe away every tear. What does this tell us about His care for His people in heaven?

   _____

   _____

   _____

2. What struggles from this life are you most thankful will be gone forever in heaven?

   _____

   _____

   _____

3. Isaiah 25:8 and 1 Corinthians 15:54–55 both speak of death being swallowed up. How does this promise give us courage now?

   _____

   _____

   _____

4. How do passages like Isaiah 32:18 and Philippians 4:7 help us understand the presence of peace in God's eternal city?

   _____

   _____

   _____

5. What is the difference between the temporary peace the world offers and the permanent peace God promises?

   _____

   _____

   _____

6. Hebrews 4:9–11 speaks of a Sabbath rest for God's people. What does that image teach us about heaven's rest?

   _____

   _____

   _____

7. In what ways does Jesus give us a foretaste of heavenly peace and rest in this life (Matthew 11:28–29)?

_____

_____

_____

8. How can the hope of heaven's rest strengthen you to remain faithful in seasons of weariness, grief, or trial?

_____

_____

_____

Epilogue

As we close this study, we are reminded that heaven is not just a distant dream. It is the promised reality of God's redeemed people. Every lesson has pointed us toward that final home where faith becomes sight and every tear is wiped away. The visions of John, the faith of Abraham, and the promises of Christ all join to assure us that our hope is certain and our future secure.

The purpose of this class was not only to inform our minds but to stir our hearts. Heaven is meant to change how we live now. When we keep our eyes on what is eternal, earthly troubles lose their grip. Our priorities shift. We forgive more easily, serve more joyfully, and persevere more faithfully.

So let this study leave you with a renewed longing for the city whose builder and maker is God. Walk by faith until that day when we see His face. The earthly journey of every son or daughter of God ends there— in the light of His presence, surrounded by His people, rejoicing forever in His love.

www.ingramcontent.com/pod-product-compliance
Lightning Source LLC
LaVergne TN
LVHW010320070426
835513LV00025B/2435